MERCY SAID

[A personal faith account of a c

May the LORD answer you
in the day of distress; and the
name of the God of Jacob
protect you always. [Ps. 20 v 1]

Rev Olabiyi Ajala
Olajala
OCT. 2021

Praise for the Book – Mercy Said No

Pastor Biyi Ajala shares a step-by-step narrative of his experience in what is akin to the valley of the shadow of death. His story, garnished with in-depth teaching on the subject of faith, speaks of triumph over the rampaging and dreaded COVID -19. Shared in this real and captivating story are profound and deep truths needed in our walk with God. "Faith in God," he concludes, "is not about when or how He intervenes but about us believing and accepting that any outcome He allows is perfect and is for our good." The book is a testament to the incontrovertible efficacy of the Word of God, the infallibility of His promises and the enduring power of His grace and mercy. Difficult to put down once you start reading it.

Taiwo Odukoya, Senior Pastor, The Fountain of Life Church, Ilupeju, Lagos - Nigeria.

Pastor Biyi tells the moving story of his decline and near-death experience as he succumbed to the coronavirus. It is a gripping story of loss, of pain, of concern for the future, all told with clarity and honesty. It tells of plans that get disrupted, and a dependence on a God who loves. It is also a story of recovery and hope, and with some great lessons learnt from the experience. In all of what he had to go through Pastor Biyi's faith and trust in Jesus shine through. I warmly recommend it to you.

Richard Wightman, Senior Leader New Life Church, Milton Keynes.

It was a privilege to be part of Pastor Biyi Ajala's care when he had critical COVID. I remember vividly that fateful Friday when blue code was called on Pastor's care. I had my worst fears as we came to the realisation that we could lose him. All we could do, at that time, was to leave things in God's hands. We hoped and believed God would stretch forth His hands and by His power give us a miracle. He did. This book, "Mercy Said No," is a must read for everyone who needs to know or be reminded that God is faithful. He is a loving Father who fulfils his promise of mercy to His children.

Adedapo Adesokan, MD/PhD. Director, Precisemed Glasgow, Scotland.

Mercy Said No is appreciated as a tribute to a unique expression of divine compassion in the context of extreme human suffering. Of the many narratives that reminisce the 2020 COVID-19 pandemic, Pastor Biyi's personal story of a triumphant battle with the virus remains significant being one of the few that views the scourge from a theological standpoint. The book emphasizes how God selectively directs His healing grace towards specific cases of invalidity; call it the mystery of divine mercy, if you like, since this grace defies human analysis and understanding. Also, the human dimension of this story draws admiration to the fortitude, courage and resilience demonstrated by the author who patiently endured unbearable pain but emerges from the encounter a conqueror by the grace and mercy of God.

Apostle Dela Quampah, PhD.
Executive Council Member, The Church of Pentecost Worldwide.
Headquartered in Ghana.

The book, Mercy Said No, provides evidence that God's power of resurrection is still available today. I have no doubt this testimony will help the faith of anyone trusting God unconditionally. Be assured, God will come through for you.

I have been friends with the author for more than 45 years. Seeing him in a videocall while he was still self-isolating at home, lying prostrate on the bed, was too much of a shock to me. I was afraid for what seemed imminent and could not hold back my tears! This was even before things got worse and he ended up on the ventilator. I cannot begin to recount how I felt on hearing this news given the stories of how narrow the chances are of people surviving this path. Thankfully, my dear friend ended up as one of the fortunate ones and lives to tell his story. I hope you enjoy reading this wonderful book as much as I have.

Chief Abiola Osho, Balogun of Iyere Kingdom, Legal Practitioner,
Lagos. Nigeria.

I am delighted by the possibility of this book knowing it is an amazing work of grace that the author, Pastor Biyi Ajala, is still with us today after his near-death experience from the raging virus that struck in 2020.

After he went on the ventilator, the only thing any of us could do to help was pray and my sister Sheila and I did daily vigils at Knock Shrine in Co Mayo Ireland on behalf of Pastor. We never gave up and even when news from the hospital was very grim, we kept going. Understandably, it is hard to concentrate on much else when someone you love and admire is so poorly. I thank God I was able to keep busy and occupy myself with my volunteering, shopping for those 'shielding' and delivery of food parcels to the needy. What a relief and what a joy when Pastor Biyi survived the ordeal. I recommend this book to you and I thank Pastor for writing it. I am sure it will inspire many to have confidence in prayer and faith in God.

Councillor Marie Bradburn, Bradwell Ward, Milton Keynes Council.

This book is a compelling narrative of a COVID-19 survivor. The powerful story told is delivered in simple, short but sometimes emotional diction and presented as a message of hope and of God's omnipotence as experienced by the author and his family. This book not only recreates an experience but also serves as an evangelical medium as it brings homethe reality of the Lazarus miracle in the bible; especially to all who followed the author's own miracle as it unfolded. Mercy indeed said No.

Yemi Edun, London based Financial Advisor & Property Consultant.

Understanding the times: A reflection on the Book

Mercy Said No

This book is not a story that needs to pass the critical assessment of the literati but one that must be followed and felt with the heart. I have known Pastor Biyi Ajala for over 30 years as a close friend and when this COVID-19 situation developed for him, I was in daily contact with his wife Esther. Later, I was one of hundreds located around the globe who gathered on ZOOM for prayer sessions as he laid in the intensive care unit. The angel of death nearly succeeded as we almost lost him.

While he laid in the hospital, I thought a lot about the upsurge of the COVID-19 virus. I witnessed a raging debate in my own church and the Church of Christ worldwide about the right response to the pandemic. Should we close church doors, or should we remain open? Opinions varied. People of faith pondered the difference between the "exercise of faith" and the "observance of prescribed safety precautions" - are the two mutually exclusive? I searched for Biblical parallel and uncovered Moses's God-ordered instruction to the Israelites (see Exodus 12:21-28). Tail end of v.22 into v.23; then v.28 is pertinent. "None of you shall go out of the door of his house until the morning. v.23. For the Lord will pass through to strike the Egyptians, and when he sees the blood on the lintel and on the two doorposts, the Lord will pass over the door and will not allow the destroyer to enter your houses to strike you. v28. Then the people of Israel went and did so; as the Lord had commanded Moses and Aaron, so they did."

To my layman's mind, there were/are parallels between foregoing 'plague' experience in Egypt and the modern-day plague or pandemic called coronavirus – or COVID-19. The parallels extend to 'administrative' instructions about social distancing. Undoubtedly, the location of 'faith' versus the need to 'practice prescribed safety precautions' when a 'plague' is in the air can confuse believers. Moses and Aaron were administrators of the affairs of Israel just as today's mayors, governors, and presidents or prime ministers are. I imagined a scenario in which a family of Israel tested their faith in God by ignoring to adorn their doorposts with blood or ventured outside with the 'faith' that God might despite His prescribed instructions protect them from being killed. In the latter scenario, the hypothetical family's disobedience would be a derivative of the absence of faith more than it would be an exercise of faith. Despite this debate, people of faith and like thereof – including pastors – died in thousands. What lessons have we learned? What was/is God saying to His church and to His anointed church leaders amid a pestilence of pandemic proportions?

And concerning the testimony of my friend, the author of this book; God chose to activate Psalm 91 on his behalf because the work and commission was/is NOT done. I also know that the hundreds of people around the world who gathered to pray and stand in the gap did not offer God empty platitudes. Each of us had an experientially specific reason in our prayers that coalesced into one core appeal: 'Lord, would you reward your servant's sacrifice of love so that he might return to your vineyard to complete the assignment to which you called him.' Pastor Biyi was spared to write this testimony and you are reading it because God's mercy said 'No' to the angel of death.

Anthony Adeola Olorunnisola, PhD.
Associate Dean of (Post)Graduate Programs & Research. Pennsylvania State University at the University Park, USA.

MERCY SAID NO

[A personal faith account of a covid-19 survivor]

Biyi Ajala

COVENANT UK LIMITED

Published by:
Covenant UK Limited

Mercy Said No. Copyright @ 2021 by Biyi Ajala

All comments and correspondence to:

Covenant UK Limited
1 Wolston Meadow, Middleton,
Milton Keynes, Bucks MK10 9AY
Email: Covenantuk.ltd@gmail.com

ISBN: 978-0-9566212-2-1

Printed and bound in Great Britain by
www.print2demand.co.uk
Westoning

Contents

Foreword by Rt. Rev. Prof Dapo F. Asaju

"Yea, though I pass through the Valley of the shadow of death, I will fear no evil: for Thou art with me." [Psalm 23:4 KJV]

Amazing Grace! This is the core factor in the wonders of nature, the complexity of human existence, the miracle of salvation and the benevolence of divine providence. It is more so, when healing miracles happen to people who have experienced illnesses which medically were considered hopeless. This book is a true story of a trying period in the life of a revered man of God who passed through the 'valley of the shadow of death' by divine help.

He has been to the edge and back; God bringing him out of the miry clay and setting his feet upon the rock - alive, well, and prospering still. This book is a compelling apologetic and evangelistic clarion call to people everywhere to 'put their house in order' in case they experience life-threatening crisis; and to be prepared spiritually to face the reality of death and eternity.

This book is a detailed account and testimony about the author's miraculous healing from the deadly coronavirus disease. Indeed, when death came calling for this 'God's General,' Divine Mercy said No!

The author, Rev. Biyi Ajala is the founder and presiding Pastor of 'Holding Forth the Word Ministry' based in Milton Keynes, UK. Amongst other compliments, he is a caring and faithful friend whose acquaintance of more than twenty years has blessed my ministry and family. A man of grace, peace, discipline, integrity, charisma, and high intellect, he no doubt comes across from this story as a courageous man of faith also.

Being the pragmatist that he is, it was not surprising to read that, facing the possibility of death, he got himself ready for heaven and concerned himself with necessary arrangements for both his family and the church! His appreciation for NHS workers is unmistakeable for their care and for their cooperation with the family in the 'journey of faith' by agreeing to read bible verses to him faithfully and constantly even when he was in coma, as requested by his wife. Everyone's faith won over fact and fear.

We learn from this book that the battles of life and the weapons we need to fight them are not always physical but also spiritual. We must therefore never give up even in the face of overwhelming odds. This was proven when the author's heartbeat stopped but miraculously resumed functioning. Why not? Brethren all over the world were on their knees interceding for him. Obviously, it stands to reason that the Lord Almighty still has need of him. His race is not yet finished neither is his course completed.

Our troubled world is still in need of the pastoral ministry and the prophetic voices of faithful men like him. Of a truth, ministers of God carry their cross and suffer afflictions too as evidenced in biblical accounts of several patriarchs, prophets, and disciples of Jesus Christ. Indeed, "Many are the afflictions of the righteous, but God delivers him out of them all." (Psalm 34:19 KJV)

This is the reality depicted in this book as the author confronts a world full of people fixated on humanistic and ungodly agendas with yet another empirical evidence of God's power and love for his own people.

It is my pleasure to strongly recommend this mini autobiography, titled 'Mercy Said No,' to all who need God to step into their life situations, as The Lord, The Saviour and The Healer.

Rt. Rev. Prof. Dapo F. Asaju,
Professor of Theology,
Bishop Theologian [Anglican Church of Nigeria] &
Former Vice-Chancellor, Ajayi Crowther University, Oyo, Nigeria

Dedication

This book is dedicated to

- ❖ All National Health Service [NHS] workers for being, in many cases, an extension of God's healing hands and caring heart. Thank you, heroes.

- ❖ My wife Esther, daughter Daniella, and my sons Emmanuel and Isaac.

- ❖ Everyone who whispered a prayer to God on my behalf. Thank you.

- ❖ The memory of my friend, Apostle Ladipo Lloyd – Kuyinu.

- ❖ The Mercy and Faithfulness of God

Preface

Despite the number of people and families COVID–19 has devastated, it is incredible there are those who still think the whole thing is a hoax and a manufactured crisis. The coronavirus disease is real and its capacity to do great damage cannot be over emphasised.

Although several public health professionals have, over the years, warned of the likelihood of a pandemic outbreak, it was disappointing the world was caught napping when it eventually happened. At the time of writing, over 2.5million people have died from COVID–19 worldwide yet there are some for whom reality of the pandemic remains a distant subject, a polarising matter and, perhaps, an overblown issue. I feel a need to share my experience of coronavirus with such people. As a person of faith, I also see the need to write this book to share with the world the testimony of how, I believe, the power of God saved me from imminent death. It is my hope that in re-living my experience with me, of walking through the valley of the shadow of death, many will be stirred in their hearts to re-examine their relationship with God and make adjustment if and where necessary.

I will not describe myself as a writer so I do not create expectations in you of a level of literary ability I cannot rise to; rather, I will describe myself as just a storyteller. I intend, therefore, in this book to tell a story. A story about a very close shave with death, a fierce but victorious fight against the deadly coronavirus and about survival and restoration through the mercy of God and the help and love of the care givers and prayerful people he orchestrated for me in my time of great need.

Strangely, I have recollections of some of the things happening to me during the weeks of being in an induced coma. I recall conversations that carried warnings, messages, lessons for individual Christians specifically and others having relevance for the body of Christ in general. Using several passages from scripture, this book reflects my inclination to show that bible narratives mirror current world events and our contemporaneous lived experiences as individuals. I am convinced the Word of God is true and, [still] relevant for today! In Exodus 33:19, God declares, '…I will show mercy to anyone I choose, and I will show compassion to anyone I choose.'

God proved this in my life hence this book. May reading it bring a fresh perspective and a deeper appreciation to you of the abundant mercies of God in your life and all around you.

While the medical staff at MKUH particularly and all NHS workers generally deserve our gratitude and praise as they have been exceptional and selfless in fighting this plague and in caring for its many victims, my faith leads me to believe that ultimately, I survived because the Mercy of God said 'NO' to the angel of death.

Rev. Olabiyi Ajala. (MTh)
Milton Keynes.
United Kingdom
March 2021

"If you would not be forgotten, as soon as you are dead and rotten, either write things worth reading or do things worth writing."

- **Benjamin Franklin**

Prologue

"And on the basis of faith in His name, it is the name of Jesus which has strengthened this man whom you see and know; and the faith which comes through Him has given this perfect health and complete wholeness in your presence." [Acts 3:16 AMP]

On the 14th of April 2020, I was admitted into Milton Keynes University Hospital (MKUH) having been picked up by Ambulance from my house and rushed to the Emergency Department. I ended up in the Intensive Care Unit that evening and thus began my month-long battle to survive the COVID–19 pandemic. I spent 22 days in the ICU, 15 of which was on the ventilator, another 8 days in the general ward before I was discharged on the 13th of May 2020.

The pandemic has affected over 100 million people around the world and has impacted many in different ways and to varying degrees. Millions have died because of this disease and, from the rank of survivors, are those who suffer from what has been termed long COVID syndrome, wherein affected people are having to deal with lingering health issues still affecting their state of physical and mental wellbeing. My case, my story is different.

I do not wish to make light of the pain of those who have suffered greatly from the effects of the virus and I am also not suggesting my experience could have served as a formula for everyone to recover. It is true there are people of other faiths and others of non-faith affiliation who came through similar or even worse experiences than mine, but this book is about my own story. It is my account of how I faced and survived the terrible scourge of COVID –19 and the role my personal faith and belief in God played in it all.

While I was in the ICU and on the ventilator, my heart stopped, and the heart monitor flattened out on two occasions. According to my consultant, both times, my heart picked up again without any medical intervention.[1] I accept medical science could have an explanation for

---

[1] The doctors concluded before this time that CPR would not be carried out on me should my heart fail because, in their judgement, such an exercise would have been futile – see end of life call in chapter 4.

what happened to me when my heart stopped and picked up again, and they may be right, but as a man of faith, I believe, right there was a divine act of God - a miracle.

I am encouraged to write this book out of gratitude to a loving God who not only healed me but has restored me back to full health, making me whole again.

"We must face today as children of tomorrow.
We must meet the uncertainties
of this world with the certainty of the world to come."
- *A. W. Tozer*

Chapter 1

He Who Has Ears to Hear

Nothing prepared us all for the coronavirus pandemic that swept the world. The disease is believed to have been first reported as an outbreak in Wuhan - China in December 2019. By January of 2020, the UK Foreign and Commonwealth Office was already advising its citizens against all but essential travel to China. By March, the number of people who had contracted the disease and the number of those succumbing to it was steadily rising.

Through travel links and connections, the disease spread quickly to several countries in Europe within a very short time forcing many states to introduce emergency lockdown measures to control the spread and transmission of this virus among its citizens. By the 23rd of March, a formal lockdown announcement in the UK by the Prime Minister shut down normal activities and altered our usual way of life. A year on from this announcement, (March 2021) it is unfortunate that normal life as we used to know it, is yet to return. With the experience of social distancing, face masks and a well-honed system of schooling and working from home subsisting for so long, the nation now seems well adjusted to a new 'normal.'

Back then, with the announcement of lockdown, my responsibility as church leader was to do what was in the best interest of the congregation members with regards to safety and wellbeing. Although government guidelines allowed for a scaled down form of church gathering and attendance so long as the necessary COVID protocols were in place, we decided we would default to doing church online by streaming live on YouTube for our two weekly meetings: prayer on Fridays and church service on Sundays.

At our prayer meeting of Friday 27th March, I recall sharing with the church a text I received during the week from a concerned individual seeking to make sense of the plague that was upon the land. The individual had asked: 'Pastor, what is your opinion on what is going on right now? Is there a link between this virus and the plagues and pestilence that occurred in the Old Testament? Or is this in relation to the "birth pains" God spoke about in terms of the signs of the end times?"[2]

It was not a strange question considering the confusion and fear we all had suddenly and painfully been thrown into. I responded saying: 'The situation is yet another saga in human history but what is happening is not primarily about the plagues or the difficulties in themselves but about a need for us to "look up." There is a need to be 'prepared and ready' in all situations and for all eventualities. Many of us were caught out in many ways[3] – financially, materially, spiritually, etc., because we dropped our guard and stopped contemplating our life and future in a deliberate and careful manner in several respects. Being the omnipotent and omniscient one he is, I believe God uses physical situations to teach us spiritual truth. The pandemic, to my mind, is a messenger of rude awakening.'

As it spread across the world, COVID–19 confounded everyone. The wise were made to look stupid and the strong; weak. Even the powerful were rendered helpless. Presidents, Prime Ministers, Politicians together with men and women of means were not spared. In every aspect of societal interaction and engagement, the virus held us all in a deadly chokehold. The world and its people lived in fear of this enemy giving occasion for men and women to consider more seriously and with great trepidation the issue of their future and their own mortality.

To this end, interest in spirituality soared and there was notable increase in sales of books that dealt especially with religion. Even Google searches on topics that had to do with 'God' and 'prayer' reached record levels in consequence. In many ways, as earlier mentioned, the pandemic was a rude awakening.

---

[2] To read up on prophecy about the end of this age, see Matthew 24 v 1 – 14.

[3] Following the lockdown announcement there was so much panic by members to stock up on food and on so-called essentials that shops had to enforce rationing measures. Generally, people have a very short-term planning mentality: coasting along with life from week to week and month to month. Companies and businesses too were unprepared for what happened when it happened. It was as sudden as the warning the bible gives about the second coming of Christ. Be prepared.

Many experts, commentators, religious leaders etc., offered interpretations about why the pandemic occurred and what its possible implication for everyone going forward could be, but I believe we are best served to understand our lives and our world only as we choose to see things from the perspective of God. God speaks to us in his word but other times in providence. This time, humankind already humbled by the terror of the pandemic and desperate, had no choice than to listen. It was an opportune moment and a wake-up call for each of us to address the important questions about the meaning and purpose of life. Why am I here? It would be of significant benefit to each of us if we would take time to re-examine our lives in contemplation of an eternity with God or one in separation from God.

For those who already have faith in God as Supreme Being, and perhaps profess a relationship through Jesus Christ, the awakening is a reminder that 'business as usual' Christianity is over. It is now time to get right and get serious with God. As the scriptures warn:

> [Luke 21: 34 -36 NLT]
> *But be on your guard. Don't let the sharp edge of your expectation get dulled by parties and drinking and shopping. Otherwise, that Day is going to take you by complete surprise, spring on you suddenly like a trap, for it's going to come on everyone, everywhere at once. So, whatever you do, don't go to sleep at the switch. Pray constantly that you will have the strength and wits to make it through everything that's coming and end up on your feet before the Son of Man.*

Being in readiness for the second coming of Jesus Christ, as the text above advises puts us, by default, in a state of alertness for any eventuality with potential to catch us napping and bring tragedy on us as the pandemic has done. The ideal of living each day as though it were the last and as though the trumpet of Christ's return can sound at any time or that death can, as a matter of fact, happen at any time should awaken our consciousness and desire to 'travel light' of baggage and offence and of the unnecessary cares of this world. A day or time of trouble does not announce itself in advance. What we as individuals can do is to be determined to live in a state of constant readiness against any of life's vicissitudes. As someone said, 'You can never be over prepared but can always be under prepared.' Wise words. Be prepared. Be ready.

What I did not realise that night as I was leading the prayer meeting was that I had, by then, caught the virus and this messenger of death was already at work in my body. Again, the imperative is for us to heed God's warning, "Pray constantly that you will have the strength and wits to make it through everything that's coming ..." Something serious and deadly was coming and I had no idea at that time how much tremor it was going to bring into my world.

What a friend we have in Jesus

One remembers the story of two sisters in the bible – Mary and Martha, who also, in their own context, had no idea about the tragic situation that was making its way towards them and would later cause them much grief and sorrow. How could they have known death was stalking their brother Lazarus? Life, it is said, is understood backwards but must be lived forwards. This is so true. How can one best prepare for everything that is coming when one can never correctly gauge the fierceness of the storm or calamity the adversary is raising against one? Make no mistake in thinking you are not in the crosshairs of the adversary because, believe it or not, you are! It is the reason the bible admonishes us:

> [1 Peter 5:8 NLT]
> *Stay alert! Watch out for your great enemy, the devil. He prowls around like a roaring lion, looking for someone to devour.*

That someone (to devour) includes you, so, "Pray constantly that you will have the strength and wits to make it through everything that's coming." And if you find yourself unable to pray when the storm or calamity inevitably breaks, be sure you know the one who can help you when you find yourself in the eye of the storm. The two sisters, Mary and Martha knew of such a person who could help them in time of need - Jesus.

Prior to this time, they had gained the friendship and love of Jesus. He was probably a frequent visitor in the house they shared with their brother Lazarus. And what a great benefit this friendship turned out to be for this family when Lazarus took ill, died after a few days, and was buried. This was a very sudden and unfortunate situation and could have remained so; but when you know and have a friend like Jesus, nothing is final – not even death, until and unless he says so.

Lazarus's sisters were blindsided by a sickness which resulted in the death of their brother; much the same way the world was blindsided by the ferocity and scourge of the coronavirus. The pandemic caused so much anguish, pain and devastation among families and communities the world over. For Mary and Martha, whilst there was yet hope, the only source of help they could think of was from Jesus. They reckoned they could count on the strength of a relationship they had formed and nurtured long before this calamity and time of trouble came upon them. The bible records,

> [John 11: 1-3 NLT]
> *A man named Lazarus was sick. He lived in Bethany with his sisters, Mary and Martha ... so the two sisters sent a message to Jesus telling him, "Lord, your dear friend is very sick."*

We must hold that thought in mind: '... your dear friend is very sick.' A friend in need is a friend indeed and there is no friend more loving and more understanding of us than Jesus. The cry for help was sent to the right person.

Though Lazarus died before Jesus reached him, he arrived at the tomb of Lazarus and demonstrated his power and authority over death by raising him back to life. Jesus, in doing this showed he had power and authority over every situation of pain, hopelessness, and every limitation the adversary can afflict us with. Including all plagues and pandemics. Lazarus that was dead became Lazarus that was raised. Why was this possible? It was possible because Jesus was their friend and friends help one another.

The factor of Jesus being their friend made the difference in this situation and can also make the difference in the life and situation of anyone who wants him as a friend. He is the ultimate game changer. His presence in our lives makes the difference between life and death, and between being lost in sin or being found by grace. Lazarus qualified for the privilege and grace to be helped because of the friendship his family had cultivated and maintained with Jesus over time. We also can partake in this grace, this fortune, this blessing. All we need to do is make room for Jesus in our hearts, in our lives and in our home just as the sisters did.

The word of God is true, and his promises are backed by his unassailable honour.

[Psalm 50:14 -15 NLT]
Make thankfulness your sacrifice to God, and keep the vows you made to the Most High. Then call on me when you are in trouble and I will rescue you, and you will give me glory.

I am with you always

On the 31st of December 2019 during our crossover service into 2020, we passed a basket of promise cards around for members to pick from as was our custom. The cards each have a verse of scripture written on them and our faith expectation is that God would providentially speak to the individual through the verse on the card. We do this to remind ourselves of how important instruction and guidance from the word of God is for our lives. That day, the verse I picked was,

[Psalm 18:28 KJV]
For thou wilt light my candle: the LORD my God will enlighten my darkness.

This was a word of promise I received from the Lord on the very first day of January 2020. As was the case with Lazarus and his family, no one in my own family could have known at that time that a major storm was gathering; one that would smash into our world in a matter of weeks. We were, like Lazarus and his sisters, completely blindsided when the pandemic broke, lockdown was declared, hospitalisation followed, isolation measures kicked in, could not reach my family and they could not reach me either etc. Yet, no aspect of this unfolding and very unfortunate situation caught God unawares because, from the very first day of the year, God had given me his word of promise that can never fail – 'For thou wilt light my candle: the LORD my God will enlighten my darkness.'

When, like Lazarus in his tomb, I was in a comatose state and completely helpless, it was the Lord (himself) who lit a candle for me and enlightened my darkness just as he promised long before the storm broke and the calamity struck. Once again, you must note that the factor of a subsisting friendship and personal relationship with Jesus brought great advantage and benefit to another family [mine] as it had done before. Sometimes, I consider whether changing my name from 'Olabiyi' to 'Olazarus' would be a fitting tribute because, like the biblical Lazarus, I too got to know what it feels like to be a beneficiary of grace: one that is unmistakable and where, indeed, "God has helped" – this is what the name Lazarus means.

But why does God show us so much kindness by helping us as much and as often as he does? Perhaps it is because of a promise such as we have noted above: "Then call on me when you are in trouble, and I will rescue you and you will give me glory." You see, God intervenes in our lives and helps us so he may show forth his power and glory through us. You may have heard it said before that great testimonies come from great trials. Yes. The bigger the challenge God gets you through, the greater the awe of his majesty in the sight of all who are witnesses to your breakthrough and your victory.

There are many people God wants to reach and the way he may choose to reach them could be through the power of an incredible victory he gives to those who, through faith in him, allow themselves to be so used. This includes you, of course. Our respective journeys towards becoming an advertisement of the power of God is never easy. Given a choice, Lazarus would rather he was spared the pain of sickness and the circumstances of dying and death. Given a choice too, I do not think I would have willingly consented to the fate that befell me and necessitated the events that have made this book imperative. But the truism holds, 'No cross - No crown.'

So, through it all, difficult and scary as it was, the power of God was demonstrated, and his glory was manifested for many to see and believe. Believe in an omnipotent God who cleanses our spirit, saves our soul, heals our body, and rescues us from all evil. I like to call this form of 'missionary outreach' the testimony of faith.[4] This is what was on display in the case of Lazarus. We are told, "...*by reason of him many of the Jews went away and believed on Jesus.*" [John 12: 11 NLT]

---

[4] Many of the health workers who attended to me later told me that my case challenged them and at least in a few cases led to renewal of faith in a prayer answering God.

This miracle of raising Lazarus from the dead was a wake – up call for many of the people of his time and God is still able to actualise this manner of 'outreach' even today by working through each of us. We are not told what disease killed Lazarus, but we all know the disease that has plagued the world for many months now. And I, for one, know the disease that put me flat on my back and almost took me out permanently but for divine intervention for which I and the cloud of witnesses of family and friends now give God glory.

But to what purpose did all these happen. So that all who have ears to hear may hear what the Spirit of God is saying and those with eyes to see may see what the Spirit of God is doing. For yet again, God is calling out to an unbelieving world that, no matter who you are, time here on earth is temporal and indeed short. Should life here on earth be truncated by any means - a pandemic, wars, calamities, etc., the reality of the hereafter should be of greater concern. These tragedies[5] are harbingers of the midnight cry that must precede the arrival of the bridegroom[6] and, as Christians, we believe they evidence the imminent second coming of Christ and the consummation of all things. Our response, as individuals, to these global disturbing and disruptive events should be for us to focus on an eternity that would matter more no matter how long, how enjoyable, and how prosperous our time here on earth is.

Jesus said,

> [Rev. 3 v 20 – 22 NLT]
> *"Look! I stand at the door and knock. If you hear my voice and open the door, I will come in, and we will share a meal together as friends. Those who are victorious will sit with me on my throne, just as I was victorious and sat with my Father on his throne. Anyone with ears to hear must listen to the Spirit and understand what he is saying to the churches."*

---

[5] Luke 21:11 (AMP) 'There will be violent earthquakes, and in various places famines and [deadly and devastating] pestilences (plagues, epidemics); and there will be terrible sights and great signs from heaven.'
[6] In Matthew 25 v 1 -13, Jesus tells the parable of the ten virgins urging that we be like the five wise ones. We are given the advice, v 13, 'watch therefore, for ye know neither the day nor the hour wherein the Son of man cometh.'

And you make a commitment of faith in Christ and say,

> *Lord Jesus, I want to accept you into my life as saviour and lord and to begin a walk with you. I acknowledge my sins and faults and believe you died to save me from the penalty I deserved and that you rose from the grave so that I also may have the hope of a resurrected life at the end of time: an eternal life with you. So, right now, I turn from my sins and open the door of my heart and life to you; be my friend now and always.*

Amen.

"I can see how it might be possible for a man to look down upon the earth and be an atheist, but I cannot conceive how he could look up into the heavens and say there is no God.

-   *Abraham Lincoln*

Chapter 2

Man Proposes, God Disposes

I really do not know where or how I contracted the coronavirus, but I realised by Sunday 29th of March, that I was not feeling well. It felt as though I had the flu. Two days before, my wife had started having an itchy throat and was coughing but still, it was one of those situations where you are in denial about the possibility of having contracted a disease which, by this time, we all understood to be very deadly. Such serious things you heard about on telly but believed happened only to 'other people'. I was still carrying on as normal. It cannot be coronavirus; or can it be?

That Sunday morning, I preached by livestream, and I remember talking about *"The Path of Life."* I was 15 days away from earning the description of being the 'sickest' COVID patient in Milton Keynes but at that moment I was still diligently on errand for the master. God was challenging both the pastor and the pastored to re-examine what the reality of what this path meant to us in this peculiar season. Were we, as a church, on the right path and walking in it? I do wonder now if God was putting me on notice then to check my heart and to put my affairs in order. Perhaps he wanted me to contemplate the matter of the Christian race like Paul did when he said,

> [1 Corinthians 9: 27 KJV]
> *I keep under my body, and bring it into subjection: lest that by any means, when I have preached to others, I myself should be a castaway.*

My understanding is that the path of life is through the word of God and the dictates of his Kingdom. Unfortunately, many have soiled their Christian testimony and derailed themselves because of careening down wrong paths in pursuit of success as the world defines it. As scripture reminds us, '...what shall it profit a man, if he shall gain the whole world, and lose his own soul? [Mark 8:36 KJV] There is no doubt we all want to do well in life but how we pursue and achieve our goals is as important as what we eventually achieve. For each of us, it is important we constantly examine the quality of our walk with God and of our commitment to doing his will. Only God can show us the path of life: one that leads to real peace, true rest, lasting joy, and good success.

Through many seasons of life, I have realised that what one needs to find the path of life and stay on it is the Word of Life itself.

> [John 17: 14 -17 NLT]
> *I have given them your word. And the world hates them because they do not belong to the world, just as I do not belong to the world. I'm not asking you to take them out of the world but to keep them safe from the evil one. They do not belong to this world any more than I do. Make them holy by your truth; teach them your word, which is truth.*

As I pondered on what God might be requiring of me, of us, by way of self-examination; I could assuredly say his grace has kept me in right standing over the years. And as far as personal and ministry integrity goes, God has also helped me. But that Sunday service was notable for me in many ways and as it turned out, it was my last outing before the series of events unfolded which brought me close to the end of my ministry assignment and my Christian journey. No wonder God was prompting a spiritual stock taking and a necessary soul check.

Down a slippery slope

From that point on, my wife and I took a turn for the worse. We were confirmed coronavirus patients. We isolated in separate rooms and our son Isaac, now back home from University because of the outbreak, took on the challenging role of caring for both his parents while at the same time needing to study to finish his postgraduate course. There was not much help from Local Health Centres because very little was known about how to treat the virus then. People were asked to stay home and not to visit the surgery and all you could get through telephone consultation was general advice that was not so helpful. Everything was bleak.

A few family members and friends became aware my wife and I were down with COVID and the anxiety and concern began to build and increase. A close friend video called me from Lagos and burst out crying. He had never seen me look as sick and vulnerable as I must have looked. I understood why he could not hold back his emotions; contracting the virus during that first wave [March of 2020] was like a death sentence.

People suggested inhalation, using chloroquine, taking an assortment of fruits boiled as a concoction, etc.; we tried them all.

The circle of concerned family and friends in the UK and aboard continued to grow. Many were calling, some at least three times a day. Though eating was difficult, some church members defied the lockdown and stay at home order to ensure they brought us food - lots of stuff. And drinks too. They would park in front of the house, drop the food packs by the door and step back and allow for Isaac to come out and bring the items into the house. Very strange and difficult times indeed. What I remember most were the blackcurrant drinks. I must have had like a thousand of those; it was as though my life depended on sucking on those straws.

Poor Isaac. I cannot imagine what his days and nights must have felt like. His siblings were far away. Daniella, his sister, in Lagos, and his brother, Emmanuel was in London where he lives and works. He had the responsibility of keeping his siblings and the growing number of very anxious people updated about how we were doing. All I wanted to do was lie down. It was difficult to fall asleep but even more agonising to stay awake!

Days passed, still nothing changed nor improved. What a life. One week passed and then a second week. We were now heading into Easter weekend of 2020. This was not the way I had planned or expected things to pan out. Of a truth, man proposes, God disposes, or as the bible says, 'People may plan all kinds of things, but the Lord's will is going to be done. ' [Prov. 19 v 21 GNT]

In January, when I was making my plans for the year 2020 and filling in my desk calendar, the months of April and May were supposed to be exceptionally busy. I had pencilled myself down to be in Lagos [Nigeria] for three weeks from the 2nd of April till the 23rd. There were two weddings in Lagos and several appointments lined up in Abuja and Ibadan and possibly a 70th birthday party in Port Harcourt. Of course, none of these plans materialised.

The month of May was supposed to have been busier. I already accepted an invitation to preach at the 60th birthday celebration of a pastor colleague in New Jersey and had planned to be away in the United States from the 8th of May till the 20th. My itinerary was to have taken me to Maryland and then Houston and Minnesota, where I was to attend a graduation ceremony before heading back home to the UK. I had bought my ticket, booked, and paid for my hotel accommodation and was just waiting for the date of departure. Everything was set for an enjoyable and interesting time abroad, but reality turned out differently; my health deteriorated, and I was sinking very fast.

On Easter Sunday April the 12th I was in no condition to attend church to preach so I sent in my letter of greetings to be read out to church members by the preacher on the day. I tried to be a part of the service as much as I could as I watched online on my phone but in bed. The letter I sent reads as follows: *Dear Holding Forth Family.*

> *It is always a thing of joy to share fellowship one with another on the platform of grace that our God makes real and tangible to us.*
>
> *Recently, I sent you a video clip announcing that my wife and I have been seriously affected by the coronavirus that is ravaging the world. I also said in the clip that we are much better albeit in the long recovery stage. Thank you for ALL your prayerful support, kindness and well wishes. I love this family. You are simply extraordinary both in my presence and in my absence for truly, this is the hallmark of true Christianity; that your faith does not lie in the power of (any) human wisdom but in the WORD of God alone. Thank you to the brethren who have helped to stand in the gap despite their own harsh realities as well. We appreciate you.*
>
> *Congratulations brothers and sisters on the glorious occasion of "Easter." Despite my present condition and pain, I have a feeling of happiness and not of sadness within me. I was asking myself why such an unnatural feeling given the circumstances. The answer I came up with is what I want to share with you. I am happy and not sad -*
>
> *1. Because there is a God Almighty*
> *2. Because he, God, knows me.*
> *3. Because I know him.*
> *4. Because his strength is made perfect in my weakness.*
> *5. Because on this Easter Morning Jesus has proven again that he is the same yesterday today and forever. It is well. I will see you soon. God bless you.*

I really thought I would see them soon, but I was wrong. As it turned out, this letter almost became, in a sense, my final official address to a wonderful group of people I had led since 2002.

It was now day 14 of me being sick with the virus and the general belief then was that after that many days, the body would have effectively fought and overcome the virus and developed immunity to start the process of recovery and wellness. This happened in the case of my wife but not mine. By now her health was improving and her strength and appetite gradually returning. She was optimistic I too would soon turn the corner and be on the mend but that didn't happen. On the contrary, I was facing the possibility of dying in my sleep and I didn't realise how precipitously close I came to the reality of that happening until one little thing made a big difference to the whole situation. That little thing is a medical device called a pulse oximeter.

*"God, who foresaw your tribulation, has specially armed you to go through it,
not without pain but without stain."*
-    *C. S. Lewis*

Chapter 3

In our Living or in our Dying

When after 14 days I had made no recovery there was much cause for concern. I had spoken to a doctor at my local surgery on the morning of Tuesday 14th but frankly, he had nothing new to suggest. According to most public health institutions, the symptoms of coronavirus included fever or chills, cough, shortness of breath or difficulty breathing, fatigue, muscle or body aches, headache, new loss of taste or smell, sore throat, congestion or runny nose, nausea or vomiting and possibly diarrhea. Although they would always admit that this list was not conclusive, it was a list of what presented the most obvious indication(s) that the virus might be present in one's body.

Of all these symptoms, it was shortness of breath and fatigue that really got a hold of me. If I had to go to the toilet, I could not bear to stand for more than a minute. When I forced myself to take a bath, it was a real struggle. I just did not have the strength nor the stamina for anything. I just wanted to fall back into bed and sleep or at least remain flat.

My wife was much better now. And with her newfound strength she took charge of what she felt I needed to be doing and who she needed to call for advice. One of our friends, a pharmacist, recommended that my oxygen level be checked but we had no means to do this at home and the friend volunteered to stop by the house later in the day to check my oxygen level with her own pulse oximeter. This device is a small clip that is often put on a finger. It measures blood oxygen indirectly by light absorption through a person's pulse. When she later used it on me, my oxygen level was 55% instead of being at least 95% which would have been normal and assuring. At 55%, I shouldn't even be conscious!

The medical term for this condition is 'hypoxemia.' It is caused by inability of the bloodstream to circulate to the lungs, collect oxygen, and transport it around the body which would explain the shortness of breath and consequent lack of strength. And what had brought this on was the coronavirus. My body was failing in its attempt to fight off the disease. On the contrary, it was the virus that was winning as it was gradually taking over of my lungs. I was literally dying by being choked and I did not realise it.

We called for an Ambulance, and soon enough a paramedic was in my home and by my bedside. She confirmed my oxygen level was way too low and proceeded to give me supplementary oxygen to enable cautious evacuation of myself to the hospital. I was very clear and lucid as she attended to me. There was no panic; not from me nor from my wife or son. An overnight bag was put together for me and as I descended the stairs, I remember giving the paramedic a hand with some of the stuff she was carrying down the stairs and into the Ambulance. These could have been my final moments in and around my home but none of us felt fear. It never crossed our minds for a moment we were about to face a major crisis and a significant test of faith such as we had never faced before as a family. Soon after, I was on my way to the emergency department of the Milton Keynes University Hospital. It was my first time in an Ambulance.

I cannot tell for sure, but I think I must have arrived at the emergency department around 7pm. The doctors and nurses though nice and comforting were apprehensive. Everyone was careful and cautious. By that time, the number of people dying every day of the pandemic was rising rapidly. The necessary filling of forms and other formalities over, one of the consultants on duty crouched low to a sitting position perhaps to be at reasonable level with my head – as I was lying down, or maybe he needed a more comfortable position for himself as he discussed an uncomfortable situation with me. I remember looking into his eyes and seeing the anguish of a man who had the uneasy task of telling yet another coronavirus patient how dire the situation was and how still undefined treatment of this disease was and how medical science could give no guarantees that there will be success of recovery at the end of trying all they knew to do. Calmly, he explained to me that I might need to be put on the ventilator and I asked him for how long. He had said to me perhaps one or two weeks and I can remember saying to him – No way!

I had read about the downside of going on the ventilator and how survival rate was barely 50 - 50. Even where the patient does survive, recovery from the process could be anything from serious to very serious. One of the nurses said to me, 'Yes, it's a very major decision to make whether to go on the ventilator or not and I would suggest you discuss this with your wife and family too.' What a kind and considerate thing to say. I was taken into the Intensive Care Unit later that evening and set up on CPAP for the rest of the night. I still needed supplementary oxygen into my system. I think I sent off a text to our family group chat late that night to appraise everyone of all that had happened since I was rushed to hospital. So much was going on all around me on the ward that night and in between frequent temperature checks, blood being drawn, and medications given etc., I think I managed to get some hours of sleep.

Putting my affairs in order

When I woke up on Wednesday 15th of April, I was a patient in the ICU. The previous day, I had been swabbed so a proper test could be carried out to confirm beyond doubt whether I would test positive for coronavirus or not. Urgent discussions still centred on the issue of my oxygen level which was not indicating acceptable saturation levels in my body even though I was being continuously helped with oxygen with the mask for breathing. I was still not doing well with breathing on my own. The doctors told me there was the possibility things may take a turn for the worse suddenly and my organs could begin to shut down if my lungs were to completely fail.

I was beginning to see the sense in what they were saying. I realised there may be no other option than the hard choice of going on the ventilator. Not today though, I told them. I needed time to put my affairs in order in case things did not turn out the way we were anticipating. I was not afraid nor was I angry at God or disappointed in his promise(s). I knew I was in God's hands and that he would do what was best for me. What came to my mind were the words of that famous hymn -***Through the love of God our Saviour: All will be well.*** The strength of faith expressed in the third stanza of this hymn is very comforting:

> *We expect a bright tomorrow*
> *All will be well*
> *Faith can sing through days of sorrow*
> *All will be well*
> *On our Father's love relying*
> *Jesus every need supplying*
> *In our living, In our dying*
> *All will be well*

I video called my family on a group call; Daniella in Lagos, Emmanuel in London, Esther, and Isaac were home in Milton Keynes. It was not a sad or depressing call. I told them I had agreed to the ventilator option and it would probably happen the next day. They asked me some questions which I answered as best as I could, and we laughed over a few things and held one another up in a very positive way. Before I dropped the call, I told them if I didn't pull through and I died, Emmanuel should have the deciding vote in all family matters. The other two jokingly asked if this was confirmation that Emmanuel was my favourite child to which I smiled and said, 'let's just say this is how I want it to be.' We all held a thumb's up sign to our phones as we said our goodbyes and I dropped the call. For some strange reason it felt more like a 'see you later' and not like a 'farewell' or 'goodbye'.

By this time, my wife, Esther already had a growing list of family and friends and church members who were praying for me. I sent out a few more texts that afternoon. As people became aware of my hospitalisation many were trying to reach me and show their prayerful support. All these gestures were much appreciated. But there was the issue of the church.

If I didn't make it, I was not overtly concerned about succession in terms of spiritual or pastoral responsibilities. That was a decision for God not me. How he would want his work to continue is something he would sort out one way or another. It was really his call, not mine. I believe the work of God is a calling which no one [ideally] takes on himself or herself. For it to be a work of grace, it must be received as a calling from God.[7] Many pastors are struggling today because man set them in office not God. I had no doubt God can and will always take care of his church.

Had I passed on, the church, understandably, would have gone through an initial time of struggle but things would have settled down eventually. I was more immediately concerned about our responsibilities and obligations to other parties. It was important we kept the financial integrity of the church intact and our commitments unbroken. With this in mind, I wrote the text below and sent it to one of the Trustees.

---

[7] Hebrews 5:4 (KJV) 'And no man taketh this honour unto himself, but he that is called of God, as *was* Aaron.'

Dear brother

I have chosen to go on the ventilator today or latest tomorrow.

Hopefully, this should be for a week or maximum two. It should all go well. Especially by the Covenant Grace of God. However, should the Lord choose that a grain of wheat is needful to die to accomplish his purpose of multiplication of "life" then to God be the glory.

The code to the safe in my office is #****#. The official marriage registry documents and such other items are in there. There is a cash sum in there that belongs to XXXX.

The key to my drawer in the office is in my black bag at home. Retrieve it and open my drawer so you can sort out any imminent issues especially banking related. There is an old paper folded but clear to read somewhere in the bottom shelf. It has the Username and password for accessing the accounts. It might take some looking through, but it is all there. Do not let the confusing way the paper looks confuse you.

Transfer the money in my publishing company account into my personal account. I am sure when Mrs Ajala receives the correct and necessary paperwork by and by, she will be able to access the money. Otherwise, yes, online access to my personal account is also written out on that funny paper. Once you have online control of the main dashboard you can navigate everything else you need to do. The card machines (readers) are well signed.

In case of my possible demise, the insurance company will pay off the outstanding mortgage amount on Holding Forth Christian Centre. This should be good news.

I will also be asking someone to do me a purchase and rent-back arrangement on my current house. I will suggest it be acquired and taken over but that my family have permanent residence there for as long as they need to but the rent for the property, while they live in it, I expect will be borne by the church which by this time will have no more mortgage burden to carry with respect to the church building itself. Okay?

My dear brother, we have come a long way and you are the best positioned under the current circumstances to understand and execute these things if need be. Thanks.

Although the brother received and acknowledged my instructions as detailed above, I would later realise he followed none of them. After I was discharged and we had occasion to talk about this and other issues, he explained he did not action any of my instructions because God gave him assurance that the ordeal was just a 'passing through' and that I would not be consumed. He was standing firm on this promise from God believing that redemption of the outstanding mortgage amount on our church building would never have to be at the expense of my life as per the terms of our Keyworker Insurance Policy. God honoured his word of assurance.

The rest of the events of that day are sketchy but the situation with my oxygen saturation level remained a concern which meant I was still having difficulty with breathing. Plans for intubation the following day were therefore to proceed.

The next day, Thursday 16th April, I remember a video call with my wife and asking the consultant to speak to her and explain what they had decided to do and to answer any immediate questions she might have; he obliged and took time to talk patiently with her. These medical workers are fantastic people. As busy and as urgent the demands on them are most of the time, they always exhibit patience and concern that makes every patient feel valued and special.

Sometime around midday, I was intubated. I don't remember if there was any counting from 1–10 but for the next 15 days, I was dead to the world.

The following pages are handwritten daily journal entries about me by Doctors and Nurses in the ICU while I was there as a patient. I am told it is usual practice for them, but I found the experience of reading through their kind words and having a feel of their warm hearts, because of the journal, very touching. I am sure you will feel the same way too. We appreciate all our NHS workers. They are, indeed, an extension of God's healing hands and caring heart.

Week 1 – In ICU

Tuesday 14th April 2020

You were admitted to our Critical Care Unit straight from the Emergency Department today. You were presenting symptoms of possible COVID pneumonitis.

Wednesday 15th April 2020

Since your admission yesterday, you have been tried on CPAP with an F12 of 0.9 and saturations in the mid to high 80s. You initially resisted the idea of intubation so we persevered with CPAP into the end of day 2 by which time you became agreeable to the idea. Your wife [Esther] was informed of this development.

Thursday 16th April 2020

Today, you were intubated to help your lungs get oxygen. Lines were inserted in your neck vein to monitor you and give you medication and fluids. We think you have corona virus but are waiting for your test results to come back.

You had an x-ray of your chest to check the lines and tubes are in the right place (they are!)

The consultant has spoken to your wife to let her know what is happening and how you are. We have turned you unto your front to help you breathe better.

Friday 17th April 2020

Good morning. It is day 4 in intensive care with presumed COVID - 19. Yesterday we put you on a breathing machine and turned you on your front overnight. This morning our orthopaedic team have been as we have turned you back on your back.

We are giving you some drugs to help your BP and watching your kidneys closely.

Saturday 18th April 2020

Good morning. It's day 5 since you have come to ITU. You currently still have a breathing tube in and are being sedated. You spent several hours on your back this morning. The doctor has just had a chat with your son — filled him in on your progress. The lock down has been extended for another 3 weeks and it is pouring with rain out there.

Keep fighting the good fight!

Sunday 19th April 2020

Good morning, it is 11am and you were turned back unto your back about an hour ago. You are still having sedation and some medicine to cause your muscles to relax so that we can ventilate you.

Keep fighting!

[15:50 hours]

While you are on your tummy, we monitor your oxygenation and you seem to prefer this position. You are on a breathing machine to give your lungs a rest and we give you medication to keep you sleepy.

I am sure you will not remember any of this; patients often have no memory of being with us. You get to miss our singing and beautiful gowns and masks. The doctor has spoken to your wife and we are hoping to video call so she can see you and pray for you. The technology does not always work well but we hope to make the call.

The team of doctors are on their way to turn you on your tummy for the night, it's now 4pm. We are giving you lots of medication to help your lungs and I really hope to see you talking to me soon.

Keep fighting.

Monday 20th April 2020

Hi Mr Ajala, I am one of the medical personnel involved in your case today. The day started with turning you unto your back since you have been on your tummy for the past 15 odd hours — not to worry, that is part of the plan. Your lungs are showing some signs of improvement as the requirements on the machine being used to support your breathing has decreased, albeit marginally.

We are optimistic and hopeful that you will continue to improve. We have now turned you unto your tummy for the 5th and hopefully last time. We will look at your numbers in the evening and decide on a further course of action.

It is getting to be warm outside and I am hoping you will keep up your fighting spirit and re-join your family soon to enjoy this summer.

Signing off for now.

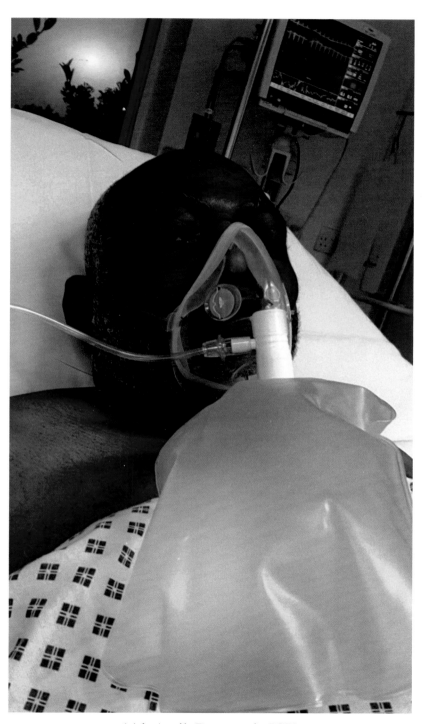

14th April. Day one in ICU

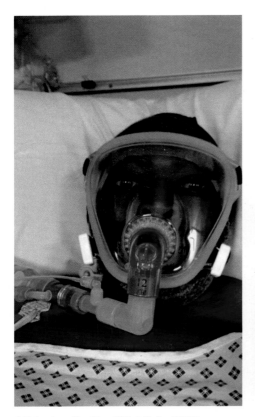

15th April. On CPAP in ICU

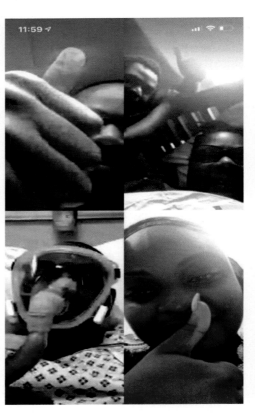

Video Call with the family before intubation. Thumbs up everyone and see you later

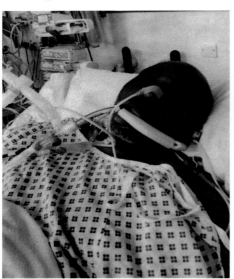

Intubated for 15 days

Dear Esther

I just wanted to let you know that the prayers and scriptures from you and the family are in place at Biyi's bedside. I hope that this provides a little comfort to you all, it certainly helps the staff to feel they are helping you and Biyi through this time. In normal circumstances there are strong connections made to support families and we will endeavour to maintain this far as we can albeit remotely.

Wishing you and your family every comfort, please let me know if I can help you further in any way.

Kind regards

The hospital staff joined us in the Faith Journey

Awake! On video call to
family from ICU

Instructions of Care.
Ward 19

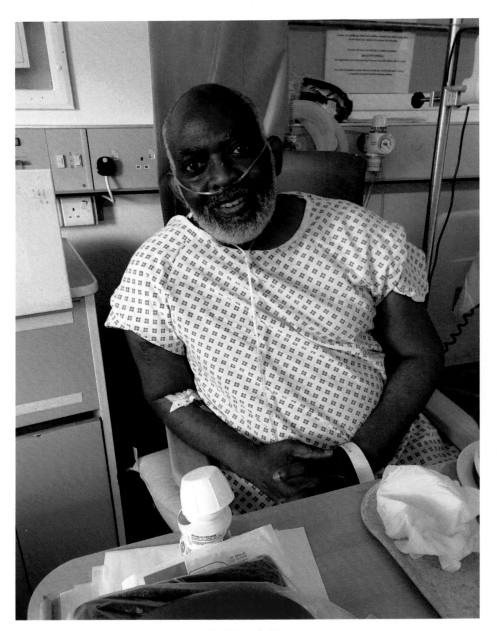

In Ward 19

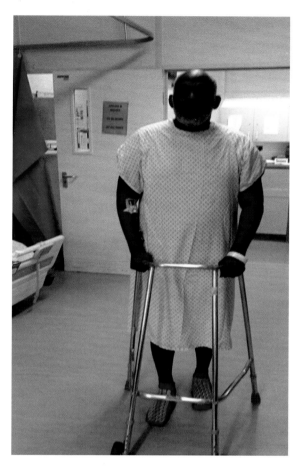

Practising walking on the Zimmer frame

Discharged and attended to by my 'angel' nurse

"Faith does not ask for any other evidence than for the written Word of God."

- *Author Unknown*

Chapter 4

Prayer Without Ceasing

I don't know what my wife did immediately after the videocall I made just before I was intubated and I have no way of knowing exactly how she felt the rest of that day, but I can imagine her being overtaken by a mixed emotion of both faith and fear. The events unfolding would, no doubt, have been terrifying for anyone. We have all experienced fear before; that emotion that overwhelms us as we face situations that threaten us, or when we find ourselves in circumstances we are not able to do anything about. Like being in a deadly storm.

> [Mark 4: 37-38 KJV]
> *And there arose a great storm of wind, and the waves beat into the ship, so that it was now full. And he was in the hinder part of the ship, asleep on a pillow: and they awake him, and say unto him, Master, carest thou not that we perish?*

In the text above, it was the disciples of Jesus who were terribly afraid. They were travelling with him and a storm arose which made it look like disaster was inevitable. They panicked. Though our contexts understandably differ from theirs, the reaction here is like what ours often is in similar circumstances of fear. Like the disciples, we sometimes find ourselves wondering and asking, does God really care? Of course, he does. Jesus' response confirms that he cared. 'And he arose and rebuked the wind and said unto the sea, Peace, be still. And the wind ceased, and there was a great calm.' [Mark 4 v 39]

Curiously though, one wonders why calming the storm did not seem to have amazed the disciples as much as the revelation that it was possible to have [such] authority or power over a natural or physical situation as a raging storm! We know this issue confounded them because, in their incredulity, they wondered, '…What manner of man is this, that even the wind and sea obey him?' [Mark 4 v 41] What Jesus did in this context was to demonstrate a dimension of ability and power which provides a teaching moment for us to learn about how our authority as believers can change our 'what is' situation into our 'what should or could be' reality.

This is a valuable lesson for anyone who expects to see the miraculous of God operate in their life or situation. Often, there are circumstances that bring fear and consternation to us yet an understanding that the power of God is real and available offers us great strength and comfort. The promise we have from God is this,

> [Isa. 43: 2 NLT]
> *When you go through deep waters, I will be with you. When you go through rivers of difficulty, you will not drown. When you walk through the fire of oppression, you will not be burned, and the flame shall not consume you.*

> [Luke. 19: 19 NLT]
> *Look, I have given you authority over all the power of the enemy, and you can walk among snakes and scorpions and crush them. Nothing will injure you.*

My wife received strength and encouragement from God in a way that must have been surprising even to her. Like Esther in the bible,[8] my own Esther proved to be a woman for such a time as this also.[9] She seemed to have awakened to a fresh understanding of how divine power and authority can be ours, as believers, over physical and non-physical situations or limitation. She rose to the challenge.

This storm must be calmed. This medical crisis and COVID emergency must be subdued. Prayer groups from within and outside the church were raised. Soon, several prayer networks around the city and the country and across the nations began to pray about my case.[10] It was incredible how this burden seized the hearts of praying people all over. The first two weeks I spent in the ICU was almost 'touch and go' as the doctors did not know at that time how best to approach this novel disease and they did not give me much chance of surviving but, I believe, the fervour of

---

[8] Esther 4:16 (KJV) 'Go, gather together all the Jews that are present in Shushan, and fast ye for me, and neither eat nor drink three days, night or day: I also and my maidens will fast likewise; and so will I go in unto the king, which *is* not according to the law: and if I perish, I perish.'

[9] Esther 4:14 (KJV) '… and who knoweth whether thou art come to the kingdom for such a time as this?'

[10] As if by divine command, my name began to show up on the prayer list of countless groups. It is remarkable how believers across the globe joined in the prayer effort for my recovery and restoration. Social media played a very positive part in making this possible.

prayer without ceasing by the church sustained me as was the case when Apostle Peter was similarly in the jaws of death.[11]

But can these bones live?

There are few situations in life that test us to the limit of our faith and, probably, of our confidence in God. We were facing one of such situations at this moment. It felt to us, as a family, as though we were right there at the valley of dry bones with the prophet Ezekiel starring down the barrel of what was, by all human reckoning, an impossible situation.

> [Ezekiel 37:1-7 KJV]
> *The hand of the LORD was upon me, and carried me out in the spirit of the LORD, and set me down in the midst of the valley which was full of bones, And caused me to pass by them round about: and, behold, there were very many in the open valley; and, lo, they were very dry. And he said unto me, Son of man, can these bones live? And I answered, O Lord GOD, thou knowest. Again he said unto me, Prophesy upon these bones, and say unto them, O ye dry bones, hear the word of the LORD. Thus saith the Lord GOD unto these bones; Behold, I will cause breath to enter into you, and ye shall live: And I will lay sinews upon you, and will bring up flesh upon you, and cover you with skin, and put breath in you, and ye shall live; and ye shall know that I am the LORD. So I prophesied as I was commanded: and as I prophesied, there was a noise, and behold a shaking, and the bones came together, bone to his bone.*

In the case of Ezekiel, what began as an impossibility was turned around on the strength of God's word. Did God care for the potential of restoration for the dry bones? Yes. Does he care about the devastation the pandemic has caused? Yes. Was God interested in a positive outcome concerning me? Yes. I believe so. In situations like this, when we are waiting on God to act, he may just be waiting on us to demonstrate active faith just as was the case with Ezekiel.

---

[11] Acts 12:5 (KJV) 'Peter therefore was kept in prison: but prayer was made without ceasing of the church unto God for him.'

'Prophesy upon these bones; and say unto them, O ye dry bones, hear the word of the Lord...' Ezekiel prophesied as he was commanded, and the outcome was a miracle.

If we believe things in the natural realm are subject to the exercise of faith in the spiritual realm and we believe the power of God is in us and at work, we can be confident of asking and receiving the desires of our heart subject, of course, to God's will. The problem with us, most of the time, is our fixation on the difficulty or challenge right there in front of us - our 'lower realities.' Don't get me wrong, I know these realities exist. They exist in the form of our storms, pain, difficulties, and hurts. We cannot deny their existence but belief in God's power helps us to look up and beyond these lower realities. With the eye of faith, we can see and function in the 'higher reality' of God's domain of omnipotence, almightiness, and possibilities.

The God who raised a living army out of a heap of otherwise dead and wasted dry bones, the one by whose authority Lazarus was raised from the dead is still available [today] to answer with mighty signs, wonders, and miracles the petitions and prayers of all those that will call upon him in confident assurance of faith.

In the middle of all the prevailing prayer and intercessions going on in diverse places, my wife received a distressing call from the hospital one afternoon. It was frankly a call to prepare her for the worst. She often recalls the memory of that call as a surreal out of body experience wherein she was taking the call in the room upstairs, but her body was somehow transported to the garden where she was pacing up and down. At this point, it seemed as though the doctors were running out of options and ideas. For family, friends, and the community of faith, it was another instance of whether dry bones can live again? Or in this context, can this particular life by saved?

The truth is, for each one of us, there comes an occasion when one must find an increased capacity of faith to keep going. By this, I don't mean faith at a usual level, but rather at the level of supernatural. The level where faith is given by God as a 'gift of the Spirit'[12]– an actualized

---

[12] 1 Cor. 12 v 7 – 11 (NLT) 'A spiritual gift is given to each of us so we can help each other. To one person the Spirit gives the ability to give wise advice; to another the same Spirit gives a

enablement. This is not saving faith or believing faith but a supernatural endowment that helps you to believe God above your usual measure or capacity. It was such grace that came upon my wife as she took this possible end of life call with the doctor.

Doctor:	*[Esther], He is on 100% oxygen support and that is giving us oxygen saturations of 80% which is low.*
Esther:	*Okay*
Doctor:	*He's also got a problem with clearing the carbon dioxide, so it is hard to ventilate him as well ... stop me from using technical terms but ...*
Esther:	*No, no, no, use technical terms because we have doctors in the family who analyse everything you say. You can give me all the figures.*
Doctor:	*Yeah, okay... so, his CO2 is 50[13] and it's really hard to ventilate him to get that down. We've been trying to do that ... so because he is now 8 days on the ventilator, he's had a period of prone ventilation which he did initially respond to but now he has had a sort of second period if you like ... I have just been speaking to the Brompton Hospital in London because sometimes they can offer, they call it **ECMO** which is where they take over the lung function by using the machine to take Co2 out and put oxygen in.*
	*Their feeling, having reviewed his case and the numbers is that he wouldn't be suitable to get **ECMO** ...*
Esther:	*Okay*
Doctor:	*... and there are no other treatments available other than the ones we are doing for his lungs.*

---

message of special knowledge. The same Spirit gives **great** faith to another, and to someone else the one Spirit gives the gift of healing. He gives one person the power to perform miracles, and another the ability to prophesy. He gives someone else the ability to discern whether a message is from the Spirit of God or from another spirit. Still another person is given the ability to speak in unknown languages, while another is given the ability to interpret what is being said. It is the one and only Spirit who distributes all these gifts. He alone decides which gift each person should have.'

[13] The normal range for Co2 in an adult is 23 to 29 milliequivalents per liter (mEq/l) or 23 – 29 millimoles per liter (mmol/l).

Esther:	Okay
Doctor:	So, I think that that is obviously as well, very worrying but we have to ask the question ... I think that leaves us without many options ... he is on his front at the moment ... if he stays as he is, I don't know how things will proceed. If he improves a bit, we may be able to get him back on his back, but he is kind of running out of options.
Esther:	Okay
Doctor:	So, what I want to discuss with you is what he would have really wanted at this point if he was here, I have some idea ... I know he didn't want to be on the ventilator initially.
Esther:	Yes. *What he would have wanted is for you to continue the treatment. That is what he would have wanted because he knows he's got a team of people praying for him to come out of this so he would want you to do everything possible that you can; keep it up ...*
Doctor:	I see...
Esther:	*... until we get that answer that's what he would want. It was that same attitude that he displayed in the beginning when he said let's just hang on with the CPAP and see if that does the job. Yeah. That's what he would want. We continue with the ventilator. We continue with the proning ... and you do what you were doing that brought those improved figures because as at yesterday, the figures – even though they were fluctuating, with the proning and the putting him back on his back, things were getting better.*
Doctor:	They were, so he's had a deterioration. It could be something that we could treat and reverse that makes that better, but I guess this far in, that is much less likely, and I think it is important that you know that there could be some reversible elements ... yeah, and we are all hoping there is. But I think we are getting to a point where there might not be.
Esther:	Okay. What I need you to do for me is I want you to have those nurses to read those scriptures over him and I want everybody

	to remain positive. I want you to remain positive with us as a family and with us as a church. Be positive …
Doctor:	I'm happy to be positive. And I also have to tell you …
Esther:	… I know, I know. You have a responsibility to inform me of the medical condition. That's fine and I can deal with that. I promise you I can deal with that. But I need for you to remain positive and I need you to assign his bedside nurses to just continually read scriptures over him.
Doctor:	Yeah.
Esther:	Can you do that for me?
Doctor:	Sorry, say that again?
Esther:	Can you do that for me?
Doctor:	We'll read the scriptures to him, of course.
Esther:	And then continue with what you were doing before that were bringing the stats up; the proning and the back and the this and the that.
Doctor:	Esther, we could do that but what I'm saying to you is that even if we did that there is a chance he might not survive and I don't want not to remain positive. I know we will do everything we can but … yeah … there is a chance he might not survive.
Esther:	Okay, alright. I hear you loud and clear. But I am trusting that you will know what to do. So that he will. I am trusting God to give you the wisdom that you need. To know exactly what to do even if it's different from something that you've done before.
Doctor:	Okay.
Esther:	Because he will survive. He's surviving. Okay? Is that alright?
Doctor:	Yeah. Esther, one of the things he said to us before we put him to sleep, I just want to check this with you, was that if his heart was to stop that he wouldn't want us to do CPR on his heart.
Esther:	Hmmmm, Okay …
Doctor:	So, that's the current status. That's his wish that we wouldn't do that, I think also …

Esther:	Can I override that wish in any way?
Doctor:	Well, it's not a decision for you or for him. I think if he had said that to me I would be saying to you now that if that happened there will be no way that treatment would work because if his heart stopped, that's really an indication he's reached the end, so the current state of having CPR is that we don't think it would work so I am sorry to say these things to you because I do want to be positive for you and I understand what you are saying but equally it is important we are transparent with you about it all.
Esther:	Yes, I understand, and I appreciate that. I wouldn't want it any other way. I like you to be transparent. I need to know exactly where he is at and what's happening.
Doctor:	Okay.
Esther:	I am fine. I am fine with you saying these things … that's the way I want it to be. For you to say these things.
Doctor:	Okay. Okay.
Esther:	Okay.
Doctor:	So, shall we see how things go over the next few hours and speak again later on?
Esther:	Yeah, that would be great. When you think it's time for me to have an update – call. I wouldn't call you because I don't want to intrude. I will wait on you.
Doctor:	Okay. Speak to you later on.
Esther:	Okay.
Doctor:	Okay. Bye for now, Esther.

My wife has always been a bold and confident person, but this was different. There was an authority in her voice and an audacity of hope that her husband was coming out of this ordeal alive and well despite the subsisting reality of his situation not improving and in fact looking worse.

From this point on, the cluster of prayer meetings multiplied and zoom prayer meetings and praise sessions became even more urgent. Throughout this period, Esther spoke to the doctors and nurses at least twice a day and with the updates she received was able to inform people on a need-to-know basis about my condition to guide the direction that praying family and friends and groups could focus on. There was a 24 - hour prayer chain by our church women and many church leaders in Nigeria, America, and across Europe led their members in prayer sessions calling on God for mercy. They were crying out that, as he had done once before, God could make dry bones live again and bring hope out of hopelessness, for with God nothing is impossible.

Week 2 – In ICU

Tuesday 21st April 2020

Good morning Olabiyi.

It is day 8 in intensive care, and you have been on your front to help your oxygen levels. You remain on a ventilator. Your kidneys and heart are stable without support. We are going to turn you back on your back this morning hopefully for the last time.

Wednesday 22nd April 2020

Good morning Olabiyi,

Today is day 9 in intensive care. Your medical team is doing a great job of looking after you. Today, you are on your back after a few days of lying on your front. We are slowly, slowly reducing the amount of oxygen we are giving you. So far, you are managing well. It is early days, but we are optimistic that we will be able to keep bringing your breathing support down.

The consultant has spoken to your wife Esther, today and updated her. I understand she has been praying for you on video calls - I am sure this brings you both such comfort at this challenging time. We hope that today we can keep things nice and stable for you and bring the oxygen slowly down. Spring has emerged outside, and you have a window opposite your bed. Have a good day.

Wednesday 22nd [23:30 hours]

Good evening Olabiyi,

I am one of the Operating Department Practitioners looking after you this evening. I have read Exodus 23 v 25 -26, and James 5 v 15 - 16 to you. We have changed your bedding and washed you whilst you were asleep.

Thursday 23rd April 2020 [15:15 hours]

Hi Olabiyi,

So far you have spent 10 days in intensive care. You are still on a ventilator for the treatment of your lungs, and you remain heavily sedated so that you can tolerate this. Your lungs are no worse today, which is good. We've noticed that you have a fever today and are trying to find out why. We changed one of the lines in your neck today, although you were unaware of this.

[15: 29 hours]

Olabiyi, I just spoke to Esther and I explained how you were and how we hoped to be able to reduce the amount of support we're giving your lungs. She asked me to read the scriptures to you and I did that a few moments ago. Be assured we are doing all we can to keep you safe. As well as me looking after you today there's a consultant and your nurse who is by your side all the time to look after you, God bless.

Friday 24th April 2020

Good morning, I am the staff nurse looking after you today.

This morning, I have read Isaiah 41 v10, Hebrews 4 v 16 and Psalm 92 v 4 to you. I will read these passages to you again throughout the day and make sure you are well looked after.

[15: 20 hours]

Good afternoon Reverend. I have continued to read the scriptures sent from your family over and over to you.

[22:00 hours]

We have given you your medications and I have read James 5 v 15 16, Psalm 107 v 20 to you. I have tapped you on your back and said a blessing over you: May you get well soon; may you get a faster recovery.

Saturday 25th April 2020

Hi and good afternoon!

I am one of the doctors on the team. You are very unwell today. Your breathing is still extremely difficult, and we are working all day today to improve it.

You seem to be more comfortable and settled when we put you back in your normal position in your bed. I gave you some medication to make sure you're settled and to control your blood pressure which was very high today.

Your dearest ones are now on the phone seeing you in a video conferencing. They must be missing you very much and caring for you a lot. You're really lucky to have them. We are working round the clock to make you better.

[Evening]

Hi Biyi,

It is day 12 of you being in the ICU and you are still unwell – coughing. Still, you are asleep from medicines to control your pain as well as help your breathing. Earlier today, we placed you on your back and the team placed a video call to your family so they could see you.

We have read scriptures to you and played worship songs near your ear.

Pastor, you have fought a good fight, you are a faithful servant and will be rewarded.

Sunday 26th April 2020

Good morning Mr Olabiyi.

You're on intensive care day 13. You're still on ventilator. You're still requiring a good amount of oxygen and still on sedation medicine. We have tried to adjust your breathing machine to help reduce oxygen requirement. We are still doing everything we can to help your breathing.

[12:45 hours]

I just spoke to your wife and updated her with your son present with her.

[13:00 hours]

You are stable, still requiring 60% oxygen via the breathing machine and sedated. You no longer need to be turned unto your tummy.

I am reading some of your prayers to you – Corinthians, Psalm 41, Genesis 2 v 7, Job 33 v 4, Exodus 23 v 25, Jeremiah 30 v 17, James 5 v 15 -16. This morning, we washed you, brushed your teeth, repositioned you so you do not get stiff or sore in the same position.

I hope we can meet and speak someday soon, but for now rest, heal and keep fighting.

[26th April 2020 Night shift]

Hi Biyi, you have two nurses assigned to take care of you tonight. Firstly, you were seen by our night-time doctors and we have spoken to your wife on the phone.

You were given a nice freshen up and wash. I read scriptures to you from Gen. 2 v 7, Psalm 66 v 19 -20, Isa. 53 v 5 and Psalm 41 v 1.

Monday 27th April 2020

Good morning Olabiyi, I am one of the doctors looking after you today in the company of some colleagues. You remain intubated still. You are also on medications that make you sleepy so that you can tolerate being on the ventilator. Each day, a member of staff reads you passages from the Bible and we are updating your wife Esther daily. You are being fed via a tube which passes through your nose down to your stomach.

You are positioned on your back today. Your blood pressure has been a bit raised, so you have been on medication to control this. You are continuing to fight, and we will continue to do our best for you.

"The best sermon is preached by the minister who has a sermon to preach and not by the man who has to preach a sermon."

- *William Feather*

Chapter 5

A Chosen Vessel

My initial sense of 'awareness' while in coma was of feeling incapacitated in movement. It felt like I had been drugged or injected with something that made it impossible to raise my hand or move my legs much as I tried. There were shadowy figures moving around me like aliens with masks. I thought I had been kidnapped by these aliens and wondered if my family members would be able to find me and rescue me. I felt I was dropping in and out of consciousness even in my unconscious state. It was like dreaming you were asleep in your dream.

I felt I was travelling in a vehicle having a form or shape like a submarine. It reminds me now of Jonah in the belly of a whale[14]. I was in a cavernous space and there was motion. We were moving across countries effortlessly and we seemed to be stopping from station to station. Or should I say, from port to port? There was this constant sound I was hearing for most of the journey which I later recognised as the sound produced by a symphony of monitors and lots of medical equipment in the ICU. There were activities happening around me on the submarine.

On one occasion, I was feeling so cold in the passenger area where I was that I was convinced I would die. I shivered for what seemed like hours and hours. It was mercilessly cold. I looked across at some co-travellers, sitting in another section, and saw that they seem to have tokens with which they could order a hot drink. They did not appear to be bothered by the cold at all. I wondered why they had privileges I didn't seem to have.

One day we got off the ship at a destination and went onshore. A passenger remained on board and I later realised he had been injected with something fatal and had died.

---

[14] Jonah 2 v 1 – 4 (NLT) 'Then Jonah prayed to the Lord his God from inside the fish. He said, 'I cried out to the Lord in my great trouble, and he answered me. I called to you from the land of the dead, and Lord, you heard me! You threw me into the ocean depths, and I sank down to the heart of the sea. The mighty waters engulfed me; I was buried beneath your wild and stormy waves. Then I said, "O Lord, you have driven me from your presence. Yet I will look once more toward your holy Temple."'

I remember saying to myself I needed to be watchful and careful as we set sail again and departed the station. I was determined to stay alive.

It is not possible to put into clear sequence the things happening to me while I was in coma. For one, time was irrelevant, distance was immaterial, location was arbitrary, and there was no real logic or rationale to the series of events as they occurred. I moved from destinations in Europe to places in South Africa and then Nigeria but no recollection at all being anywhere in the UK. When I came round though, the doctors were quick to remind me that I was in Milton Keynes Hospital, and had, in fact, not left my bed for weeks! This was the fact physical evidence presented no doubt, but the [true] reality was that my spirit was alive, alert, unhindered and roaming free.

I recall being caught up in the middle of a war. An armed conflict reminiscent of guerrilla wars that happen in real life. It was brutal and many people died but when it looked like we were going to be overrun and captured, help came from an army that was like a Peace Keeping Force and they rescued us. I don't know who we were fighting and why, but I was glad the good guys showed up. I can still feel, even now, the same sensation of relief and excitement I felt when help showed up as we faced that desperate situation. I cannot say whether the time I was engaged in this battle, down under, coincided with that time in the ICU when doctors were thrown into serious panic because of a sudden and unexplainable turn for the worse in my condition. Going by what one of the nurses who witnessed it all later told me; It was crazy. It is impossible to know if what I was experiencing in my other world had anything to do with what was going on in the ICU world, but I was glad help came, one way or another, and I survived both battles. Mercy said no.

Before this time, I had been to South Africa only once. My wife had business to transact there, and I decided to tag along and experience the much talked about country. It was not a particularly remarkable trip so why it featured as one of the memorable places I can recall visiting while I was in coma surprises me. But I can remember meeting with different people who needed guidance, direction, and encouragement about many issues of life. Someone needed advice on family/relationship matters involving marriage, the pros and cons of a planned emigration, etc.

Another family was dealing with how to cope with the normal struggles of life along with the reality of caring for one of their children who had a compelling medical need. So many people with many issues to which I gave godly counsel as I believe God gave me wisdom to impart. I could somehow relate this experience in a sense to that of Paul.

> [Acts 16:9-10 KJV]
> *And a vision appeared to Paul in the night; There stood a man of Macedonia, and prayed him, saying, Come over into Macedonia, and help us. And after he had seen the vision, immediately we endeavoured to go into Macedonia, assuredly gathering that the Lord had called us for to preach the gospel unto them.*

On reflection, I believe, somewhere in the realm of the spirit, I was still at work for the master: he was using me to speak into people's peculiar circumstances by offering them help and direction through godly wisdom and counselling. Through the medium of what you and I would describe as a dream encounter, our spirit man is able to receive information from another spirit being. I may not be able to confirm the fruit of this labour, but it suffices me to know that somehow, the purpose of the Almighty is served and that someone somewhere in South Africa woke up with answers to their issues. What left the most lasting impression on me, though, of all my memories from the weeks I was in coma was when I believed I was in Nigeria.

All that time I was in coma, I had a form of consciousness that made me know I was incapacitated and in bed, yet I was active enough to experience different scenarios and engage with different people. At some point after South Africa, I found myself in the University town of Ile-Ife in South Western Nigeria. This was the University I attended for my first degree and from where I graduated in 1983. For some reason I was back in that town. A play written by an academic and priest was being staged at a popular venue in the town and the title of the play was 'Opomulero'[15] – The pillar that sustains the house. It was the story of a man who would not succumb to the power of death because he was upheld by the power of God.

---

[15] "Opomulero" is a Yoruba word. Yoruba is a language spoken most prominently among the people of South Western Nigeria. It is the mother tongue of the author.

The event was well coordinated and much advertised throughout the city because it was to be an opportunity for evangelism also.

I was in the auditorium along with many others who had come to watch the play and there were several officials in white cassocks there to facilitate the programme, announce the play and coordinate proceedings. As I settled into a comfortable position, a young man approached me and greeted my familiarly. I apologised that I did not recognise him. He then told me that many years ago, I brought great joy into his life because I gave him a gift that meant so much to him. He was grateful for the opportunity to say thank you after such a long time. He was with his family and he gladly introduced them to me. I think the lesson here is that the good we do in this life is undoubtedly never in vain. Maybe someone needed to hear this as an encouragement.

I wanted to buy a copy of the brochure for the night's event, but I remembered I did not have my wallet on me. It is amazing how clear in one's mind, fact and non-fact can be, even in such a state of unconsciousness. Somehow, I knew I was a hospital patient and that I did not have access to my wallet or money. I called the attention of a young lady who was one of the ushers and told her I would like to have a copy of the brochure so I could read details about the play but that I had no money to pay for it. She smiled at me warmly and greeted me familiarly just as the man had done earlier.

Again, I apologised that I did not know who she was. She told me she was a student at the University but was volunteering to help the organisation behind this evangelism outreach. She told me she knew of me because her parents are well acquainted with me and had always spoken highly of me about how helpful I had been to them and that frankly she would not be where she is today if it had not been for the help people like me rendered to her family. She then told me who her parents were. She also said I did not need to pay for a copy of the brochure because they were already paid for by a charity organisation supporting activities that promote evangelism. I collected a copy and thanked her.

While everyone seemed to be getting ready with one thing or the other, I found myself near the author of the play and engaged him in discussion about the storyline and what was the core message he was trying to communicate to the world. He told me he received inspiration to write the story of a man whose life, strength and renown was tied to his source – God, by reason of his faith in and commitment to Jesus Christ. This man therefore was someone who was unflappable and untouchable by any force or weapon of the evil one including the clutches of death!

In a sense, it was a humanised story of how God, at work through Christ, having ultimate authority and power over sin and death, can make his divine advantage work in the life of any man or woman who would trusts in him completely. I remember looking him in the eyes and saying, 'Jesus Christ is either master of ALL or he is master of none; Right'? He nodded in approval and smiled as though he was happy that I caught the revelation he was trying to make me see. I left him and settled back unto my seat and waited for the play to start.

For hours and hours, the play did not start. Nothing meaningful was happening except the sound check going on and the light casings being rigged into position and the musicians tuning their instruments and the hall gradually filling up and later becoming full but still, everyone was busy with activities and the priests and actors etc., were pouring through sheaves of paper and everyone was getting ready to get ready to get ready to get ready....

I think I slept off as did many of the people who by now had filled the hall. When I woke up from my sleep, I felt I heard the voice of the Lord say to me clearly,

'This is exactly what my church is doing out there in the world. The church is preoccupied with activities. The people are in position and waiting for the salvation message of Jesus – The Pillar That Sustains the House! But my church has preoccupied itself with everything else but that which should matter most – The Salvation Message.'

It was as though I could feel God's heartache and pain. For all those hours of waiting in great expectation for the play to begin and for this message to be proclaimed in art form; nothing happened. Sadly, such is the state of the church today - full pews but empty pulpits. Empty of the truth of God's word and of the power of conviction his word brings. We are a people who have allowed ourselves to be sold on counterfeit values but must now seek repentance as we re-align ourselves back into God's purpose as we reorder our priorities. We need to make the main thing the main thing! The salvation message of Jesus Christ is simple and devoid of all the complications we have submerged it under.

> [John 3:16 KJV]
> *For God so loved the world, that he gave his only begotten Son, that whosoever believeth in him should not perish, but have everlasting life.*

> [Acts 2:21 KJV]
> *And it shall come to pass, that whosoever shall call on the name of the Lord shall be saved.*

> [Acts 4:12 KJV]
> *Neither is there salvation in any other: for there is none other name under heaven given among men, whereby we must be saved.*

> [Acts 16: 30 – 31 NLT]
> *"...Sirs, what must I do to be saved?" They replied, "Believe in the Lord Jesus and you will be saved, along with everyone in your household."*

After I received that message, the scene changed to the venue of a prayer vigil that was being organised by a local church. I seemed to have arrived at the venue earlier than the church leaders and organisers, so I was waiting together with a few others who had also arrived early. We were told the leaders and organisers had to go to various homes and other places to bus people to the prayer meeting. And so, we waited and waited.

The pastor of this church is someone well known to me in real life. Finally, when he showed up and the prayer meeting started, it was more like a social gathering than a church meeting. It had the feel of a situation where many of the young ladies had been bussed in from the University hostel under the pretext of attending a Christian religious event, but the organisers knew that they had other thoughts and plans in mind; thoughts that were far from anything spiritual or divine! We are warned,

> [2 Tim. 2: 19 AMP]
> *"... The Lord knows those who are His," and, "Let everyone who names the name of the Lord stand apart from wickedness and withdraw from wrongdoing."*

It was hard to watch what was unfolding in the name of Christ amongst those who are supposedly called by his name. I believe God shared these revelations with me because he has a message for the world, and he conscripted me and has taken me through an experience that might give me a platform to share these things in the hope that this opportunity might help fulfil the prayer of the man who realised his need of salvation too late but pleaded that somehow others who still had such opportunity to hear and change be warned unto repentance.

[Luke 16:27-31 NLT]
'Then the rich man said, 'Please, Father Abraham, at least send him to my father's home. For I have five brothers and I want him to warn them so they don't end up in this place of torment.' But Abraham said, 'Moses and the prophets have warned them. Your brothers can read what they wrote.' The rich man replied, 'No, Father Abraham! But if someone is sent to them from the dead, then they will repent of their sins and turn to God.' But Abraham said, 'if they won't listen to Moses and the prophets, they won't be persuaded even if someone rises from the dead.'

This book in your hand is an exhibit of the mercy of God in action. Its contents echo, yet again, the truth that God's word is real. The message underscores the urgent need for us to turn away from our indifference to sin and from wickedness and evil in our hearts and lives. We need a heart of repentance and one that is willing to accept the saving grace in Christ Jesus especially now, when we still have opportunity to do so. And for those who have done this,[16] we must strive to run our Christian race with merit and purpose, observing to do the will of he who has accepted us and called us into service in his Kingdom.

If you would take these words seriously, the entire ordeal, of having been so painfully conscripted by God, in order to bring this message to you, would not have been in vain.

---

[16] John 1 v 12 – 13 (NLT), "But to all who believed him and accepted him, he gave the right to become children of God. They are reborn – not with a physical birth resulting from human passion or plan, but a birth that comes from God."

Week 3 – In ICU

Tuesday 28th 2020 [04:30 hours]

Good morning Olabiyi, I am an Operating Department Practitioner here at MKUH and one of the people included in your care. This is the second night I have spent by your side. Keep up your inspirational fighting spirit so that we can get you better and with your family. I am looking forward to seeing you better! My best wishes and prayers for you.

[16: 35 hours]

Dear Bi,

I am your nurse today. I started at 07:00 hours and will finish tonight at 20:00 hours. I came in this morning and you were quite heavily sedated so I stopped all your sedation to see what you will be able to do. You started opening your eyes and was coughing a bit more.

After 2 hours of the sedation being off, you managed to squeeze hands and move your toes which was very good. During that time too, your wife called, and I have given her an update. Unfortunately, at 11:00 hours we had to sedate you more because we had to move you to ICU3. Having said that, you were just lightly sedated, still eye opening and coughing a lot.

You did very well throughout the day. I managed to wean your support from the ventilator. The plan for you before was that we might have to put a tracheostomy on you ... but the way that you are going at present, we might be able to remove the tube and extubate you ... this is good news. Hoping for your continued progress.

[Tuesday 28th April 2020 Night Shift]

Good evening Mr Olabiyi, you are still slightly sedated and do open your eyes frequently. We gave you a good wash so you can enjoy your sleep. I read few scriptures for you so you can have a blessed night -

Isaiah 40 v 10, Exodus 23 v 25 - 26, James 5 v 15 - 16, Psalm 41 v 1, and Psalm 27 v 13 – 14. Hope you get well soon!

Wednesday 29th 2020

Good morning Olabiyi, I am one of the doctors looking after you today. You've done really well over the last few days and we have reduced the amount of breathing support you require from the ventilator. We have also reduced your sedation and you are opening your eyes frequently; we are updating your wife with your progress daily and she sends her love. She is praying for your recovery. I have read you Genesis 2 v 7, Exodus 23 v 25 -26, James 5 v 15 -16, Psalm 46 v 1 with best wishes.

Thursday 30th April 2020

Good morning Bi,

I am one of the nurses that have been looking after you. This morning you have been opening your eyes to voice and we have been reducing your ventilation settings getting you ready slowly for extubation. You seem very comfortable today. Your scriptural prayers have been read to you this morning. Keep getting better and we are all looking forward to you recovering very soon.

[10:45 hours]

Hello Olabiyi, I am an ICU doctor, but I have not looked after you directly before now.

I have heard however about how you have been whilst the team here at MKUH have looked after you. It sounds like you have been very unwell but have progressed well in the last few days.

You are now on your back, the breathing tube is still in, but the ventilator is having to do less work for you. We all hope we can take the breathing tube out soon. Keep your spirit up. All the best.

[Nightshift 23:00]

You have two of us as nurses taking care of you tonight. I have not seen you before, but I have to say you look better now than in the picture of you taken in the earlier weeks; that's an improvement. You're asleep right now and there's all sorts of beeping going on, but good lights are showing on your monitors.

I'm sure you'll do well and look forward to that day. Goodnight.

Friday 1st May 2020 [10:00 hours]

You are more awake today; we have communicated well – you are helping by not pulling on your tubes. We are waiting for the doctors to give us a plan for today. It is nice the sun is out today as it has rained for the last 2 days.

[14:30 hours]

We extubated you this afternoon. Your family has been updated by the consultant. You are still weak but today has been good. Keep working hard.

Saturday 2nd May 2020 [10:00 hours]

Good morning,

I am back again as your nurse. You are looking much better today, and your voice is getting stronger. We are going to sit in a chair today.

Good morning Pastor Ajala. This is your consultant doctor. Today is day 19 on the ICU and yesterday was a good day as we were able to get your breathing tube out. We are all so happy as we know that only one week ago you were so sick! Today we are going to call Isaac and Esther while you are sitting in the chair. Keep up the good work.

[16:00 hours]

ICU video-called son and wife. There were some technical difficulties with the sound but Mr Ajala's son and wife were still able to see him and speak to him. Patient happy and waved back. This was followed up by a normal telephone call with wife and son.

We removed 2 lines this afternoon and you managed to have sips of water. Really well done! We are going to try yogurt for dinner.

Sunday 3rd May 2020

Dear Bi,

Today you continue to make progress. We are needing to give you less oxygen and we hope to transfer you to a normal ward soon.

You have made excellent progress and it is great that we can start your rehabilitation process soon.

We had a video call with your family yesterday.

Monday 4th May 2020

Good morning Bi,

Today is a sunny Monday. It is your 21st day on our Intensive Care Unit.

We have taken out the tube from your lungs a few days ago and we are very pleased to see how good your progress is. If everything remains stable and you keep recovering well, we aim to send you off to the wards this week.

You are doing super well and smiling away. Keep it up! Lots of love. Spoke to Esther. She's doing well, they all miss and love you lots.

You asked about your friend who lives in Nigeria, you would like to video call him, I will discuss this with Esther and the doctors. Well done.

Week 4 – Moved to Ward 19

Tuesday 5th May 2020

Good morning Mr Ajala, you are doing very well today. You had a difficult night as you couldn't sleep but you seem to be enjoying the sunshine we are having this morning though.

Your strength is increasing by the day and we are happy that you can go to the ward now.

One of the Emergency Department doctors that saw you when you were first admitted into MKUH is visiting with us today. He was extremely happy to see you again in a much better state.

Very sad to see you go but equally very happy that you are ready to begin your next step of the journey to full recovery. I will make sure you're in good hands on the ward.

The journal entries stopped when I left the ICU. I thereafter spent 8 nights in ward 19 before I was discharged on Wednesday 13th of May 2020.

"Never be afraid to trust an unknown future to a known God."

-    *Corrie ten Boom*

Chapter 6

As For Me And My Household[17]

Esther Ajala [Wife]

I must start by saying I did not find it easy to write about this very dark period in my life. To gain perspective on some aspects of what he wanted to write about in this book, my husband Biyi, would ask me questions. But every time he would ask me to fill in a gap for him, it takes me back to a place I do not want to revisit. Covid-19 rocked my household. Biyi has invited us to join him in sharing our story with the world through the medium of this book. My three children and I would therefore be writing about what that stormy period meant to each of us and how we coped with the terror of an unknown outcome. What immediately follows is my own story.

Two days after lockdown was officially declared, I noticed I was having an itch in my throat. At the time I didn't pay much attention to it but by the weekend I was beginning to feel worse even though I still assumed it was just a touch of flu. Out of an abundance of caution, I started self - isolating in a separate room. Unfortunately, the 'Flu' got worse; I started to cough, my body was racked with pain and I had a nasty headache. The pain was so much that after a week I called my Dr to ask for stronger pain killers as paracetamol didn't seem to help. I told him I had the flu and he asked me a few questions which I answered despite the coughing fits. He stated, 'You have Coronavirus.' I was in denial and it took him a while to convince me. I was a little shocked. Really? My temperature hadn't been excessive as I had been checking it with a thermometer.

By this time, Biyi had some discomfort but he wasn't really coughing. We figured I had transferred it on. What do we do? Well apparently, you have to wait it out for 14 days and then you feel better. In the meantime, you drink various concoctions, take paracetamol (my Dr had upped mine to Cocodamol), steam your airways with menthol and sleep. That should sort it out. I had never felt so ill. I was extremely tired, had lost my appetite and the pain all over my body was excruciating. I found it

---

[17] Joshua 24: 15 [NLT] '…But as for me and my family, we will serve the Lord.'

difficult to get out of bed. It was so bad sometimes I couldn't walk to where Biyi was and might not see him in over 24 hours.

Predictably, I started to feel better after 14 days and my strength was gradually building back up. Unfortunately, as he has described in a different section of the book, this was when Biyi's situation necessitated that he be rushed to hospital because his breathing difficulties continued. As difficult as they were, the past two weeks of pain were nothing compared to the next four weeks we faced.

As they took him away in the ambulance, my mind and heart was bombarded with all kinds of thoughts. First, the house felt empty. I couldn't think straight. I couldn't sit down. I paced the sitting room and started to tremble from a chill that seemed to spread all over me from the inside. It was as if my physical body was not in agreement with my mind. They seemed to be going in opposite directions ripping me apart in the process. I needed to get a grip and pull myself back together. There were many things to be done: his family in Nigeria needed to be told; my family needed to be told; church leadership needed to be informed; a statement needed to be issued to the church; ministry friends needed to be informed; his close friends and associates, the list was endless. Where do I start?

I needed to sort my emotions out first so I could attempt to think straight. So, I had a heart-to-heart talk with myself. I said to myself: 'Esther, as a Christian, you keep going on about faith so where do you stand? Do you have faith that Biyi will be coming back home? Make up your mind now. If you believe it, stand firmly on your belief and do not be moved.'

I made up my mind, settled my thoughts and stuck with the decision. Biyi was coming back home. I trusted God to do this. It was sealed. Now I could get to work.

I set up a group chat for his family in Nigeria so I could give them information collectively and so we were all on the same page. I identified one of his brothers that I could share the difficult 'stuff' with. Someone needed to be in the know. I created a general message to go to church leaders and the women's group.

That first night, we were told he would be placed on a ventilator and his chances were 50/50. For some strange reason, I took that to mean that he had a 50% chance of the ventilator working to overcome Coronavirus. I didn't associate it with survival. Unbelievable.

Biyi did not want to go on the ventilator. He wanted to stay on the C-Pap but as this was not improving his situation at all, the Doctors were concerned for him and were having stern words with me urging me to get Biyi to give consent to going on the ventilator while he still had capacity to make this decision. I went into panic mode especially as Biyi, at this time, seemed more concerned with tidying up his business affairs and passing on passwords and instructions to his associates! He said, 'I'm a practical man. If I don't make it, I need to put things in order before I go.' The Doctors were not impressed, and neither was I! Go where?

By the next day, and after many discussions with and explanations from the medical team, he was placed in an induced coma and put on a ventilator. My head was in a spin. My mind was foggy, and it seemed like I was in a daze. I was trying to hang in there and I dug deep into my spirit to find a place of rest and be at peace.

My days changed. A new routine was established: Prayer meetings, explaining, communicating with those who needed to be in the know, updating, answering questions from concerned friends, asking questions from my back-up medical experts, calling the hospital, researching, booking appointments to speak to Drs in charge, video calls with ICU, carrying the families along- trying to keep their spirits up and so on. I got to eat lunch sometimes at midnight when the day was over.

There was overwhelming love and support from all at home and abroad. The call for prayer went out and the response was incredible. The news went viral. Pastor Biyi had Covid and had been put in an induced coma in ICU. The women's group in church set up a 24-hour prayer chain that remained unbroken for weeks. Many pastors locally, nationally, and internationally were praying for his recovery. The church leadership also set up zoom prayer meetings and we met a couple of times a day.

Over the next few weeks, I believe God protected my mind and emotions many a time when I spoke to the hospital and as I dealt with the whirlwind of activities around me.

I tried to carry everyone along as much as I could. It was tiring. It was overwhelming. I struggled to keep up. Then there was that niggling thought at the back of my mind... Would he make it? I kept pushing the thought out of my mind and did everything I could to remain positive. Of course, he would come home. Every time I climbed the stairs in our home I would look towards the bedroom and say out loud, 'You are coming home mate! You have a church to run. Come back and carry your load.' Then I would laugh. I was storming hell's gates and knocking on heaven's door. We will win this battle.

I arranged a praise session thanking God for his healing. Let's praise God on credit! The turn up was incredible. We didn't have enough room on Zoom. We thought we could accommodate 300 but apparently, we had capacity for just 100. Oops! It filled up by 3 minutes after the hour. Holding Forth Church choir did a wonderful job, and I asked a cousin of mine, if he wanted to sing. He responded with; it has to be the song 'Breathe' by Dunsin Oyekan. I had not heard the song before then but from that day, after he sang it with his guitar accompaniment, it became my anthem. My confidence that God would do it grew. I noted that at every difficult moment on this journey, God gave me a Word, a song or revelation or understanding that gave me hope. There were other songs that kept me going.

As the days went by, there wasn't much change in his condition, but the doctors were ready to give it a few more days before reviewing options. Pages of scriptures were passed on to ICU alongside the family pictures and I asked that they be read over him daily. Every phone call started with, 'Have you read the scriptures yet?' Doctors soon knew about this and would start the conversation with, 'I just finished reading the scriptures to him,' before they gave me the medical report. Eventually the stats improved, and we were all encouraged.

Then, the call came.

It is called the pre-death call apparently. It was a very negative report. The only positive thing that I understood was that he was still alive. I was told that morning that, 'Biyi had a rocky night.' The word 'rocky' took on a new meaning. He was being moved for a scan/MRI so they could see his lungs and have a clearer picture of the state they were in as they couldn't get oxygen into his lungs. When the results came back, I was told that the virus had completely taken over his lungs. I was offered a video call so I could see him. I rejected it because it felt that acceptance of the call would be acceptance that I wouldn't see him again. I said to the doctor, 'Not today, maybe tomorrow.'

I was offered the services of the hospital chaplain and if I wanted the chaplain to read the scriptures I had sent in... all the indications were negative. But I earnestly asked for the scriptures to be confessed over him. I told them it didn't matter if the staff reading them was a Christian or not; I just needed for the words of scriptures to be spoken over him as often as possible.

I had arranged another praise session for the next day but wondered if he would be alive by then and, if he wasn't, would it be necessary for it to hold? The children called and said the praise session should go ahead even if their Dad didn't make it as that is what he would have wanted. We kept on praying. This was a critical time for us all. For some time, I had been meditating on Psalm 46 v 10 'Be still and know that I am God.' I held on.

On the day of the Zoom praise session, I watched the clock all day long and kept my phone free for calls from the hospital. When they called, they had no good news. The doctor only wanted to know what I thought Biyi would have wanted at this point as they had done everything they could but the situation was not improving. I thanked the medical staff and asked that they keep on fighting for his life and that we were praying for him and for the entire medical team for them to know what to do that will be of benefit to Biyi because, he will be coming home.

The Praise session held. I was very tense but got through it. Another 24 hours passed. There was no change. What was God up to? I kept on listening out for the still small voice that would give me some hope or some answers. God didn't fail me and spoke in various ways: a phone call, a prayer, a word of encouragement, a song in my heart, a song on YouTube. We all held on. Finally, light began to appear.

The change came. Slowly but surely the figures began to improve and there was a repair of all the damage done to lungs, kidneys etc. God had done it. We all heaved a sigh of relief. He was coming home.

In life, we go through many tests to build up our character and faith. I hope I passed this test as I never want to sit it again. As a family, our faith in God became stronger and we became even more close-knit. Each of my children went through various struggles and drew closer to God as we passed through this ordeal. I know the testimony of Biyi's recovery has been an encouragement to many people who have found themselves trusting God for [almost] impossible things. Without a doubt, God is faithful. May our stories continue to bring encouragement and strength to all around us.

On the 13th of May 2020, after being in Milton Keynes Hospital for exactly a month, a small crowd gathered outside of reception at the hospital to welcome Rev Olabiyi Ajala as he was discharged. We are very grateful to the wonderful NHS staff who had worked so hard to save his life and for the mercy of God that said 'NO'. He came home.

Daniella Ajala [Daughter]

I was in Nigeria when the coronavirus pandemic broke out and was cut off and far from the rest of my family in the UK.

As the whole world began to grapple with the reality of the pandemic everyone was trying to make sense of a situation that was not making much sense. Many people, especially in Nigeria, believed the disease was a fabricated lie and at the onset not enough care and attention was paid to public health warnings until casualty numbers began to rise. I was trying to figure out what this development could mean for me.

Because of an existing medical condition my Mum was particularly worried for me and called me very often. That was until she herself became unwell having contracted the virus which forced her into self-isolation.

I remember calling home one evening to check up on Mum and Dad mentioning he was not feeling at his best. I responded jokingly stating "oooooo looks like you got the 'rona". Although he dismissed my fears then, a few days later it had become obvious whatever was wrong with him was serious. Both of my parents had the coronavirus, were seriously ill, and here I was thousands of miles away from them. Being the first child and the only girl, I was used to looking after everyone in the family making sure everyone was ok. This time, that task fell on the youngest in the family – Isaac, who had to step in and take charge and for which I always say well done and thank you.

Mum improved after 14 days as medical experts suggest should be the case with many people. By day 16, she was on the road to recovery. Dad on the other hand was still very ill. Early one evening, I got a phone call from Isaac that things had taken a turn for worse, and that Dad had been rushed to A & E in an ambulance. Something to do with his oxygen level being very low and him needing help with breathing. I really cannot describe exactly how I felt at that moment, but I knew I didn't want to be in Lagos. I had never felt so far away from my loved ones as I did that day. I needed to find a way to get back to the UK.

I began to try desperately to get out of Lagos. National lockdown meant airports in Nigeria were closed and flights in and out of the country prohibited. The hours were long and the days difficult. That sense of helplessness was almost paralysing. It was hard not to cry a lot.

The day after he got into the hospital Dad agreed to be intubated and put on the ventilator. After he consented to this, Dad video called the family to inform us of this development. It was both a relief and an apprehension to see him. I remember the boys really trying to make the conversation light-hearted by cracking jokes. Emmanuel said something like "okay Dad, this will be a good time to get some shut eye and rest. Rest well… but don't rest too much because we want you back." I remember everyone laughing but honestly, I didn't find the situation we were in funny at all. I was thinking, will this be the last time I hear his voice? Dad, I looked forward to you walking me down the aisle. So much still ahead of us, Dad. He was on CPAP with an oxygen mask which he put on his face on and off as he made conversation. This was hard.

I remember Dad looking at the screen as everyone was laughing and saying, "Daniella doesn't find it very funny guys." He probably does not know this, but at that point I was actually crying.

Dad was so unwell and the report out there about the rate of fatality among coronavirus patients was very dire. The great encourager that he is, Dad gave a thumbs up sign, and we all did the same. It was our unspoken way of promising each other we would stay positive. That was the last time we spoke to Dad before he went under.

So much uncertainty so many unanswered questions, I needed to go back home. I needed to be with my family.

After several emails, calls, and a visit to the British High Commission, I finally got on the waitlist of people trying to get back to the U.K by evacuation flights. I am glad Mum was able to keep me fully in the loop. She recorded as much as she could of her conversations with the hospital, so I had constant updates even though they were sounding worse every day. Dad's oxygen level was not getting better, and we were told at some point he seemed to have had a heart attack. We were given a timeline by the doctors: they explained that if they didn't see any improvements in 2 weeks, they would need to re-evaluate the situation. No improvement over that time, they reckon, might be an indication that Dad wouldn't recover, and the ventilator would most likely be turned off. This was a lot to take in because we were now past day 10 and how much could we hope for in just 4 days?

I remember falling on my knees to pray and asking God if my father would make it through and live or not. Every time I prayed though, I felt God was telling me again and again, 'There is nothing that happens that escapes my attention.' I was comforted by these words. I knew God was aware of everything that was going on and that whatever happened, God was in control.

After Mum got the 'end of life' call, I had a meeting with my siblings and later with Mum that the planned zoom praise scheduled for later in the day should go on regardless. My siblings and I concluded that even if we got word that Dad did not make it through and he passed before the scheduled zoom praise meeting, it would have been what he would have wanted: for the meeting to go on as a gesture of gratitude to God whom he had served with all his life and might. The meeting went on as planned. Dad survived the imminent crisis.

By the time I was on my way back to the UK, Dad was out of coma but still in the ICU. He was not out of the woods yet, but things were finally looking up and God was showing himself true to His word. Yes, He was in control and by all indications Dad was getting better. It was very nice to be home and with the family.

The next few weeks were of deep gratitude to God; my father was moved out of the ICU into a general ward and was finally discharged from hospital. It was a slow road to recovery, but I am so thankful to God for his ever-present help in time of trouble.

Emmanuel Ajala [1st Son]

It was a painful reality when it became obvious that Mum and Dad had contracted coronavirus. I live and work in London so the only way I could follow up with what was going on back home in Milton Keynes was by phone. Lockdown measures were in place and sadly, there was little I could do from where I was: a situation I so desperately wanted and needed to change but had no control over. I never felt as powerless as I did in that moment.

Then, one evening, I was told that Dad suddenly had to be rushed to the hospital because his condition was far too grave to be managed at home. What was happening? This is Dad we are talking about. My Pops! I could not make sense of it all as the situation escalated far beyond my imagination. Nothing prepares you for a situation like this.

The day following his admission into hospital, I sent a text to him very early in the morning hoping he would have the energy to reply. It was a text with a message one wishes could carry every emotion one was feeling in the heart and convey every thought in one's head. However, no words truly captured what I felt or thought. For, if you were about to lose a loved one what would that last message look or read like? What can one say? These are questions no one should [ideally] be put in a position of having to answer.

I sent the text anyway, every line written with deep meaning as I considered the joyful years behind us and contemplated the hopeful ones ahead of us: all the plans and events to look forward to, for him and for us as a family. I needed him to know he had to pull through this with all the will power in him and with everything he had. To my surprise, my father's reply was short and somewhat vague. His reply to my long and painful text was simply this, *'God will be glorified.'* That was all. I was annoyed and perplexed by the brevity of his response. I was looking for a message with a bit more fight, a bit more hope and didn't feel I got that.

Later that day Dad video called us to say he had agreed to go on the ventilator because his oxygen saturation level was not improving, and the doctors advised that this was the best option given the circumstances despite the inherent risks that come with this procedure. At that time, the chances of surviving coronavirus while on a ventilator were slim. The facts and statistics we were up against were not encouraging at all. We held together as we spoke to dad on the videocall that afternoon and believed for the best in the face of all the odds.

On Thursday 16th April 2020, Dad was put on the ventilator and in induced coma with no guarantees of him coming out of it alive. In the next couple of days and weeks we kept holding on to hope. It was all we had. I prayed to God to spare him, but it seemed as though his condition only worsened.

I threw myself hard into exercising and running. I ran, ran, and ran some more! It cleared my head and to a certain extent helped in lifting the weight of the situation off my mind as my thoughts became clearer as soon as I hit the pavement and ran a couple of miles. I prayed every mile and wishfully dedicated each mile to my Dad's recovery.

I thought possibly, through the power of God, my accumulated strength and health could be shared with him in some way. A crazy thought, I know, but you would be surprised at the thoughts that go through your head when you are desperate for a miracle. I was desperate for one.

As days dragged into weeks, there was very little good news from the hospital for us to hold on to, but we chose to stay in faith and hold on to God. When Mum told us about the possible 'end of life' call, my siblings and I spoke and advised Mum we were in favour of continuing as we had been doing – trusting God and praying, nothing changes. As a family, we were in touch with each other often not minding the physical distance of where we were location wise. We still tried to uplift one another sharing some laughs and managing to crack some smiles. Dad had always taught us not to fear death and often said whenever he died, we must not cry. We were ready for whatever God had in store for our father, whether that meant him coming back to us or passing on to glory. Glory?

Yes, glory. I remembered the last message my dad sent to me. Short, brief but now having more meaning to me. Dad said, *'God will be glorified.'* My siblings and I had the same understanding that regardless of the outcome we would continue to give God all the glory. Glory for the time we had with him. Glory for the many lessons we learned from him. Glory for the quality of life he lived and the love he showed, not just to us his family, but to all who knew him. Our father has always been an advocate for making ready a people prepared for the coming of the Lord, but little did we know that along the way he prepared us as well, for any and everything – even death, if, and when it comes.

I am most glad and grateful that my Dad survived this attack. We can glorify God through him living, not passing. Many people are inspired by the testimony of what God has done for Pastor Biyi and for us as a family. Thank you everyone. We truly serve a God who answers prayers.

Isaac Ajala [2nd Son]

With the formal announcement of lockdown in March 2020, I arranged for a cab to take me back home to Milton Keynes from Leeds where I was on a one-year MSc programme in Law and Finance at the University. Because of the volume of [Uni] work I needed to get done before end of summer, this turn of events was already a major disruption to my plans not to talk of the scarier things that were to follow.

The thought of lockdown and the hysteria about a pandemic was the least of my worries at that time as all I could think about was the academic workload ahead of me: upcoming exams, 4,000-word essays to be written, a practical group project and a 10,000-word dissertation. Adding to the pressure I was under was the underwhelming prospect of finding gainful employment in what was an already difficult job market and economic climate. By this time, I had already invested a huge amount of time and energy into the possibility of what comes next after my studies and now came the complications of COVID.

I had been home for just over a week when my mother took ill. And she got it bad. Waking to the sound of my mother almost coughing life out of her lungs and seeing her writhing in pain forced me into more care-giving tasks than time enough to focus on my studies. Sometimes, I doubted she would in fact pull through, but I prayed; I prayed she would overcome this sickness that had brought my energetic and vibrant mother to such a weak state. It was when she began to turn the corner of recovery though that things took a turn for the worse for my father who by now was also sick but not with symptoms as obvious as that of Mum.

My Aunt was like an angel sent from God bringing food, groceries, and meals to the front door to support me in the care of my sick parents making sure however that she kept due protocols of safety. The first two weeks were very hard, looking after my parents with the thought of either or both dying a constant possibility. All this time, my phone was a hotline from family and friends wanting to know what was happening with them and from too many people giving me too many instructions on what to do! What a time.

Dad felt tired all the time, his room neighboured one of the bathrooms in the house but to make it from his bed to the bathroom and back certainly looked as though he had just finished from running a marathon! I remember, I think it was the day before he went into hospital, I often made fruit concoctions for inhalation for both, but Dad really did not think it was helpful to him and cared less about it. So, this night, about 9pm, having finished my daily grind needed to stay on track with my studies, I prepared the concoction for Mum. At just about midnight, Dad sent me a text as I was about to sleep. He was having a rough night and thought inhalation could make things better for him. I was dead tired but even before I finished reading his text I was on my way down the stairs and to the kitchen to make him what he wanted.

It was the very next day that a series of events led to Dad being taken away to the hospital. The hospital told us a few days later that medical examinations seemed to indicate Dad suffered a minor heart attack at some point while still at home. My mind tells me it was probably that night when he strangely requested for steam inhalation at a very odd hour. I cannot stop wondering what could have happened had he not asked me to help him out that night, in consideration of how late it was, or if he had sent the text but I pretended not to see it until the next day? I get the chills just thinking about how our decisions to do or not do, to go or not go, can ultimately be the difference between whether we live or die, whether we win or lose.

I am thankful God gave me strength to carry out the responsibilities I needed to perform throughout those tough and horrible weeks. To the glory of God, Mum continued to enjoy good health and Dad make a remarkable recovery. And me? I finished my MSc programme with distinction and God rewarded me with a good job before the end of Summer 2020 in one of the big 4 accounting firms in the UK.

At home with my family on the day I was discharged. Acknowledging well-wishers from afar because of social distancing.

Resting. Eating. Resting. Practically living in my recliner chair.

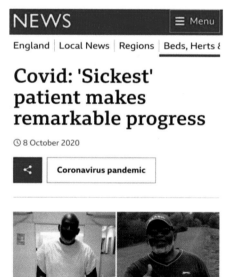

Headline coverage on BBC Online News

Live TV Interview on BBC News

On one of my rehab walks with Emmanuel

Striking a Pose! Last day of August 2020 having done at least 90 mins of walking everyday.

Minor hall roof caved in completely.

On the 2nd June, a section of our Church Building collapsed.

Debris from collapsed hall being cleared.

Officiating the commital to earth of my friend and colleague.

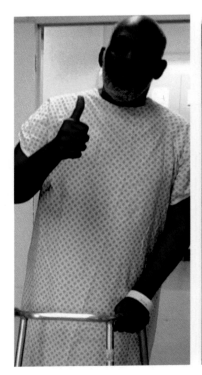

"Olazarus." Now an avid long-stretch walker. God of Miracles!

Still on errand for the Master!

"The way to grow strong in Christ is to become weak in yourself."

-   C. H. Spurgeon

Chapter 7

A Bruised Reed, A Smoldering Wick[18]

My gradual awakening from coma came in the manner of hearing little instructions from the nurses. They would ask me to wiggle my toes, squeeze a finger or nod my head if I could. I could, so I did. They were testing to see how much of my cognitive and physiological abilities were working correctly. I remember a nurse asking me if I wanted her to read my prayers to me and I shook my head and must have had like a horror look on my face which must have surprised the nurse. I did not know my wife had sent them several bible verses which these angels had dutifully laminated and which, as you can see from the journal entries, they read to me without fail almost every day in my greatest time of vulnerability and helplessness. I didn't know all that.

She asked me if I wanted her to read the bible passages to me and somehow, in my head, I was thinking, 'why does she want to read me the last rites?[19] I am not Catholic, and I am not dying!' Sometimes, we think we know what is best for us but how wrong we often are. Prayers and daily reading of scriptures had saved my life. I was just coming out of 15 days of darkness and what provided light for me throughout the long night was the very first thing my logical mind was telling me to refuse. Typical man, 'They claim to be wise, but they are fools' [Ro. 1:22 CEV]. I must have confused that nurse, but she did well in hiding her bewilderment.

At that time, I didn't know for how long I had been in coma and exactly what the state of my health and the condition of my body was. But I felt very weak and fragile. The nurses had put pictures of my family above my bed and as soon as they could they were asking me questions to confirm if my memory was intact or impaired.

---

[18] Isaiah 42 v 1 – 4. Although this prophecy references the Messiah directly, it also speaks concerning those who, though weak in themselves, are nevertheless valuable and useable vessels for Kingdom purpose and assignment. By the power of God, a broken reed can still be repaired and a smoldering wick, can still be ignited! I am still available for the Lord's work!
[19] The last rites are a religious process for cleansing one of his or her sins before they leave this earth. A rite more usually practiced by Catholics.

I recognised Esther immediately in her Mrs Doubtfire [red] glasses in a picture we took in Spain. We had travelled with the boys to Barcelona in December 2019 in what could have been a trip of a lifetime if I had not made it through this ordeal. I guess that 'trip of a lifetime' is thankfully still ahead of us. Because of the mercy of God, my family can still look forward to more memorable things to do and trips to make now that I have a second chance on life.

I recognised all my family members in the pictures the nurses showed me. They asked me more questions and I was able to answer back as much as my very low and faint voice allowed. My memory was intact, and my mind was clear; you could tell the nurses were very happy about this. Fantastic people these nurses.

Understandably though, my voice had been affected because of the intubation experience and it did take a long while for me to be able to speak and be heard clearly. But it was good to be alive. The hospital staff arranged for me to have video calls with Esther and Isaac as soon as I could and what a joy to see their elated and joyful faces. They could not hear me because I was still very tired and weak and I could not speak up, but it was comforting enough that they saw me and with the help of the nurses, I was able to wave to them before we dropped the call.

We had come through a major part of surviving this deadly coronavirus attack and I was determined to get back on my feet as soon as possible. I told one of the nurses, "I am going to come out of this, and I am going to run in a marathon." She didn't laugh, I guess she felt that would have been unprofessional, she just humoured me by saying, "Good idea, but let's get you to the point where you can stand on your two legs first." Of a truth, at that time, I did not even have enough strength to turn or pull myself up in bed. But I kept this goal to run a marathon in mind as the future I saw for myself – one where I was well and able and physically fit. It took me a while, but I got there faster than medical science could have predicted.

I was moved into a general ward and a different set of care workers took over. It was nice but somehow, I miss the angels that worked in the ICU. This was different. It was noisy and busy, and I found it difficult to sleep. And maybe because I was by now more cognitively aware and alert, I started to long for home. I still could not function independently and needed assistance with everything, but I was getting fed up with being in hospital over such a long time. I was on the ward with a few other people. The amazing thing about the people I was with though was that somewhere in my 'yesterday' I was sure I had encountered them. There were these two patients on the ward who were not as fragile and handicapped as I was and as the gentleman next to me was. The man next to me had also just survived COVID but his daughter who was admitted at the same time as him did not survive. He learnt of this painful news only after he came out of coma and was in recovery at the ICU. What a sad story.

The other two men in the room with us made conversation a lot. But it was all such a déjà vu experience for me. It was as though I had experienced ward 19 before I encountered it. In another dimension, I had heard all their conversations before and several things that played out in that room were things I was already familiar with. I know what I am saying may not seem to make much sense, but I assure you I was not out of my mind! Not then, not now. I believe we are all more spiritual than physical beings even though we hardly realise this. I also believe it is possible to discern things in advance when we discipline ourselves to be more sensitive to the spirit of God. There are many events in our tomorrow that God, in his omniscience, can make known to us in advance. Examples of this abound in scriptures and they confirm that God truly knows the end from the beginning just as he declared in his word – "Only I can tell you the future before it even happens. Everything I plan will come to pass, for I do whatever I wish". [Isa. 46: 10 NLT]

What he planned was for me to survive COVID and upon surviving, I am certain his wish is that the testimony of this occurrence be declared as evidence of his faithfulness, kindness, and love to as many people as possible. Although this story is a personal account of my experience and therefore subjective, nothing in it is exaggerated or embellished for the sake of creating a fantasy or for self-glorification.

Rise Up and Walk

The process of regaining strength was very slow and gradual. I still had an oxygen line connected to my nose, but it was now more out of caution than of necessity. By this time, I could go on a little longer without the line and I would not be desperately out of breath. I still had it in place for most of the day and through the night though. I pretty much still needed help to function and get things done but I was bored of being so weak and helpless. A team of physiotherapists came to see me to talk about how to prepare myself for rehabilitation. I was asked to stand up with the help of a frame and this was when I realised how much we all take for granted when we get up in the morning, swing our legs off the bed and just get up and go! Having been through what I have been through, I promised myself never to take anything about being healthy for granted again.

I had to learn how to feed myself all over again. To coordinate the action of lifting the spoon from the plate and into my mouth was difficult. Being weak and vulnerable is a humbling experience. Some of the [black] health workers in this ward knew who I was; that I was pastor of Holding Forth the Word Ministry in the city. Some of them attend churches where their pastors had encouraged them to pray for me especially in those very dark days of being in coma. And now, they were encountering me in the ward. Seeing the man of reputation and prestige 'out there' now 'in here,' on his back and not even able to wipe himself. There is another life lesson here; about how quickly our pride and ego disappear when we are faced with the reality of our puniness. Be humble dear brother or sister. After all is said and done, you are a mere mortal; an individual, not any more or any less than the next person. I also learnt a lesson here about what a fully surrendered life looks like.

Many of us who sing *'all to Jesus, I surrender, all to thee I freely give...'* have no idea what this means. Not until you are so weak that you cannot lift your hands or legs and therefore must surrender yourself fully to someone else's care are you able to appreciate and understand how far we are from what God expects of us in terms of a submissive life and surrendered will. For many, although our confession echoes surrender, our will is still unbending, unyielding and very un- surrendered.

We are like the little boy scolded by his parents for standing up in a moving vehicle and was told to sit down. He does as he is told and sits down but then says to his parents, 'I am still standing up on the inside.' Many Christians are like that, outwardly we cut the image of surrender but inwardly we are not surrendered. For me, it took an ICU experience to understand the mystery of what Paul learnt about surrenderthrough his own experience of weakness.

> [2 Corinthians 12:7-10 TLB]
> *... I was given a physical condition which has been a thorn in my flesh, a messenger from Satan to hurt and bother me and prick my pride. Three different times I begged God to make me well again. Each time he said, "No. But I am with you; that is all you need. My power shows up best in weak people." Now I am glad to boast about how weak I am; I am glad to be a living demonstration of Christ's power, instead of showing off my own power and abilities. Since I know it is all for Christ's good, I am quite happy about "the thorn," and about insults and hardships, persecutions and difficulties; for when I am weak, then I am strong—the less I have, the more I depend on him.*

The true strength of the Christian man or woman is in a surrendered life. As a patient, I realised that the more I surrendered and let the care givers do their job, the better things were for me.

It is the same with our Christian life. The more we allow God to work in us and with us and we do not frustrate his grace with our human understanding and efforts, the more productive and successful we will be in all our endeavours. I cooperated as much as I could. It was not easy, but I did. Especially as I was hopeful that soon, I would be strong enough to go home.

I was now two days in ward 19 and it would be my daughter's birthday in two days on the 9th of May. She had just flown into the UK from Lagos, from where, alone in isolation, she had endured the fear and uncertainty of whether I would live or die. She would later talk about the confusion she faced when packing for her trip; whether her choice of clothing should be for a wake-keeping and funeral service or for a thanksgiving service. The UK government had begun to arrange evacuation flights out of Lagos, and she had been fortunate to finally get on one. I was silently hoping I could be home in time for her birthday which would have been nice, but this was not to be as the relevant medical officers did not think I was ready for discharge yet. I did not like the decision, but I understood and accepted it.

Essentially, I would not be considered ready to go home until the relevant medical care groups approved that I was in a state where I was not a danger to myself or a significant burden to anyone else. Because of the nature of my trauma of having been in intensive care, with significant loss of muscle power in my arms and legs, it was crucial from the viewpoint of the physiotherapists, especially, that I was mobile enough to move on my own and climb a few stairs on my own as well as be able to stand unaided for a while without the need to collapse into a chair. They had to tick me off as 'able' in these basic test areas.

They came to see me on Thursday 7th May. This was just before the May Day Bank Holiday which was moved back four days for the whole of the UK from the traditional day of celebration on Monday to Friday. The holiday was moved so it would coincide with the 75th anniversary of VE Day; a celebration that marks the day towards the end of World War Two when fighting against Nazi Germany came to an end in Europe. It was going to be a long and lonely and boring weekend. Bear in mind that throughout the period this pandemic has raged, no family and friend visitors were allowed for patients on admission at the hospitals. It was tough.

By the time the team of physiotherapists left me on Thursday, the most I could do was stand with the help of my Zimmer frame after being helped up. I would then shuffle sideways to sit on the chair next to my bed. More sitting than lying down during the day was recommended at this time. I was determined to use the entire weekend to improve on my ability to move more and become sufficiently mobile. I would encourage myself to shuffle to the toilet to take a leak and graduate from using the bottle. At least, the idea was to give it a good try.

Although the toilet was just about 40 paces or less from where my bed was, I started out towards it on one occasion but could not make it past the door that leads out of the ward. The nurses' station was right outside this door and one of the nurses stopped me from going any further.

Seeing how unsteady I was on my feet; she could not risk me having a fall and injuring myself. Quickly, she brought the wheelchair around and pushed me all the way to the toilet. At least I was out of the ward and in the toilet and, though with a lot of clumsiness and difficulty, I could get the business done by myself. I was working hard on regaining some privacy and personal dignity. And by pushing myself to walk and shuffle more, I was starting to strengthen my weak muscles.

I started using the Zimmer frame more and more. First learning to pull myself up from a sitting to a standing position, resting a while, and then slowly moving up and down and around the ward as much as I could before I ran out of breath and strength. Thankfully, my efforts paid off. By Monday 11th of May, I was needing the Zimmer frame less and less. Even the nurses at the station were surprised every time I walked past their station heading for the toilet. I was winning. By the time the team of physiotherapists came back to see me on Tuesday 12th I was walking slowly but well enough. And because my other health statistics were also indicating positive outcomes, I was told there was a possibility of being discharged that week. This was good news, but I still had to pass the staircase test.

Wednesday 13th May was a week since I was moved from the ICU to Ward 19. It was exactly one month to the day I was admitted to the hospital and now it was looking like the day I would be discharged. Everything hinged on the final report of the physiotherapists, and it was down to the stairs test. I was wheeled to a vantage point and asked to walk up the stairs. All I could think of at this time was home. I want to go home. I needed to be back with my family. I must pass this stairs test. I got up from the chair with care, got myself steady and ready, held on to the bannister, placed my right leg on the first step and pulled myself up. Next, I pulled my left leg up and above the level of my right leg and pulled myself up again as I climb the second step. I climbed the third and the fourth in similar manner and the next and the next and the next.

By the time I got to the first landing they reckon they had seen enough of my ability to climb. They were not even expecting that I would do it in progressive climbing style as I did. They would have been content to see me pull myself up unto a stair, level with both feet first and rest before attempting the next stair and the next till I got to the landing, but

I just literally marched up the steps all the way to the landing. I guess I was hearing an inner voice saying, "In the name of Jesus Christ of Nazareth rise up and walk,"[20] and I simply obeyed.

What God did for me in the 8 days I spent in Ward 19 was a continuation of the wonder of his great mercy on me throughout the entire hospital experience. It was difficult for most people to believe that the man who, a little over two weeks ago was fighting for his life, is now recovered enough to be on his way home. It was an anxious wait before all the paperwork for my discharge was finalised so while I sat down by my bed side waiting, I had time to reflect on the last 30 days. It was all down to God and God alone.

That morning I had made my way to the bathroom and had given myself a wash. The shower was hot because I wanted it so and I enjoyed the spray on my face and my body, and I spent a long time just having the water run all over me from head to toe. Absolutely refreshing. It was my first proper bath in 30 days, and I was having it unaided. I am alive and well. I was not quite there yet physically, but even at that time, I could think of millions who have not been as fortunate as I have been.

I went back to the ward, put on a nice tee sheet and a comfortable pair of trousers. I dabbed myself with a nice cologne, sat back in my chair and waited. This was the first time I would be in my own clothes since I arrived in hospital a month ago. I was feeling more like the old me now: not like a patient but like a person. I was feeling more and more excited as the activities of the day unfolded and my discharge was imminent.

One of the angels from ICU had rearranged her schedule so she would be available to help me out of the hospital by wheelchair. It was a moment she had believed and hoped for. She saw it all. The crisis, the anxious moments, the miraculous turnaround, the first signs of awakening from coma, the first video call to the family, the recovery in the ward, and now she, on behalf of her colleagues, was completing the joy they all felt for me by taking me to meet up with my family and friends and church members who by this time had crowded the hospital entrance ready to welcome me back from the dead. The joy of an

---

[20] Acts 3:6 (KJV) Then Peter said, Silver and gold have I none; but such as I have give I thee: In the name of Jesus Christ of Nazareth rise up and walk.

occasion which, had it not been for the Lord's mercies,[21] could have been otherwise.

> [Psalm 124:6-8 KJV]
> *Blessed be the LORD, who hath not given us as a prey to their teeth. Our soul is escaped as a bird out of the snare of the fowlers: the snare is broken, and we are escaped. Our help is in the name of the LORD, who made heaven and earth.*

When the nurse pushed me to where Esther was, she and my wife hugged. They had become acquainted because of the video calls when I was in the ICU. The nurse could not help herself as she wiped her eyes of tears brought about by the emotion of the moment. This was not a nurse just doing her duty, this was one human being genuinely happy for a fellow human being. We hugged as she turned to make her way back to face the rest of her busy day. She is Asian, I am African but that never mattered; she truly cared. She had seen a miracle of God and was grateful for the mercy she knew God had bestowed on me, my family and the community that were at that reception area that evening. Thank you, angel.

---

[21] Lamentations 3:22-24 (KJV) *It is of* the LORD'S mercies that we are not consumed, because his compassions fail not. *They are* new every morning: great *is* thy faithfulness. The LORD *is* my portion, saith my soul; therefore will I hope in him.

"The future is as bright as the promise of God."

- *Adoniram Judson*

Chapter 8

My Redeemer Lives

Earlier, on the day of my discharge, Esther had sent word out to friends and church members that I would be released from hospital sometime later in the afternoon and that anyone who was available to be at the hospital entrance to cheer and celebrate the victorious result of what many of them have been fasting and praying about could come to the venue. Many did.

As soon as I was wheeled out and they all saw me there was a chorus of cheers and loud clapping and from somewhere in the ranks of the members a chorus of praise singing rang out. What a joy. These moments, as with everything in our contemporary world, were captured on camera and in no time, had gone viral. I waved and nodded to people gathered and thanked them for their love and sacrifice and the honour showed me by coming out to see me leave the hospital. Soon after, we were on our way home.

There were a few people who went ahead to the house to await my arrival and yet others who got to the hospital after we had left the premises and then decided to head for the house too. Everyone respected the social distancing rule but the celebration and congratulations still reflected the joy and elation in the heart of us all. In the words of the psalmist, 'This is the Lord's doing; it is marvellous in our eyes.' [Psalm 118 v 23 KJV]

My family and I stayed outside the house for a while to appreciate all the love and solidarity people had come to show us. The neighbours on our street were also magnanimous in their warmth towards us. Families to which we have long been neighbours but never really interacted, overcame their cultural stiffness and were genuinely happy for us. It was good to be home.

There was a lot to catch up on and so many people to thank. As I settled into a comfortable chair I turned to Isaac and said to him I would like to record a 'thank – you' speech and have it sent out on social media platforms. People who had waited for this testimony needed to see it.

I was mindful of the fact that I was still quite fragile and my voice, especially, was still raspy and low but I gathered my thoughts and started speaking into the camera. I said,

Hello,

> *My name is pastor Biyi Ajala. Many of you know me as pastor of Holding Forth the Word Ministry in Milton Keynes, but many more know me as a name on your prayer list. Many of you have not met me but you have engaged dutifully in interceding on my behalf. I want to thank you very much for allowing God to use you.*

> *I was discharged from hospital today, got back home today and I just want you to know that I am so grateful to everyone that took up the mantle of prayer and the burden of praying and interceding which is why I am here today.*

> *So many things went wrong, and many things could have gone differently, but there was a switch; a definite, definite point that God's hands moved on our behalf just because you prayed. We are not glorying in the fact that our hands and our ability has achieved this, that's not what it is about. It is about us going to God, ... 'if my people who are called by my name...', that word is still true. As many times as we approached the throne of grace, God is willing and ready to hear us. I want to thank you. Many of you I don't even know. Across the nations people have overwhelmingly showed love and support for my wife and for my children.*

> *I was mentioning earlier today that a very high point for me was when my wife got the distressing news that it looked as though I wasn't going to make it and she had a meeting with all the children and the children decided that even if it ends today, we will still go ahead with the praise session we had arranged because that's what dad would have wanted. The faith, the conviction, the lack of fear, the belief..., you know, and trust in Almighty God; I could not have asked for a better legacy. What am I trying to say? God has been good to us. God has shown us once again that we can say, 'our fathers trusted in you and you came through for them, and you delivered them'.*

> *The testimony of what God has done, the testimony of me coming through to you, the testimony of being able to talk to you as I am doing right now, is an encouragement, a faith anchor for very many situations in life.*

I've got people who approached me on the ward and they just talk about how, they don't know me but that my story has challenged them, my story has awakened faith in their personal lives and I know that this is just the beginning. I can only say that you are part of that story. God is asking us to retrace our steps. One important message that I have come back with is to retrace our steps. It is for us to leave aside those things that don't matter. It is for us to make the main thing to be the main thing. And I hope that together, we can work further on making ready a people who are prepared for the coming of the Lord.

Once again, thank you for your goodness and your kindness and for standing with us in prayer. My wife, Esther, my daughter Daniella, my sons Emmanuel, and Isaac all send their love and their gratitude and their appreciation. The Lord bless you. Bye-Bye.

As soon as this clip was released the reaction was immediate. Texts and phone calls and enquiries started pouring in. My family began to joke that I was now a celebrity. I was just grateful to be back home. I looked around my house and my surroundings. I was beginning to appreciate things anew. Things I had lived with for so long and had taken for granted. The smell, the feel, the peculiarity, and comfort of your own home. We take these things for granted. Most of what we did for the rest of that day was take phone calls. As people could not physically visit because of the lockdown regulations my wife was endlessly on the phone assuring people that yes, I was back home and yes, I was doing okay. To God be the glory.

That night, we all got very scared. At the hospital, monitoring my oxygen level was constant since it was important to see that my lungs were gradually improving in their functioning capacity. So, before I turned in for the night, I used the pulse oximeter to check my reading and it was in the mid 80s. This was not good. I was uncomfortable with the reading but did not want to panic my wife and children.

I checked the reading a few more times but the results did not show improvement over the initial level it indicated. I reluctantly mentioned the situation to my wife, and she did not surprise me with her reaction. She was immediately on the phone to the hospital and was told that if there was someone to bring me in, I should be brought back into A & E. I refused her suggestion and entreaties though. I was not going back into hospital. I knew what the pulse oximeter was reading but I was sure within me I was not in a declining state of health. I wasn't going back into hospital again so soon. I just could not handle the thought.

She could not force me, so she left it at that. Daniella was worried too but she understood with me, Daddy's girl. It was one of the scariest nights of my life: would I die in my sleep if the level dropped further? There was no way I could get a mask and an oxygen bottle at home should one become necessary. Had I been too eager to leave the hospital without being quite ready? At some point in the middle of all the fears and questions weighing on my mind, I fell asleep in a sitting up position. Thankfully, I was still alive in the morning.

It was a very slow path to recovery. My oxygen level picked up after that first night. I checked it at least two or three times a day for several weeks. I was mindful of my sleeping position most nights to give myself the best opportunity for my lungs to function better. Medical practitioners tell us the prone position is best for this. This means lying on your front. I still could not hold my bladder well at this time, so I had a constant need to go to the toilet which disturbed my sleep quite a lot. My finger grip was weak, and I could not hold a pen properly nor write legibly.

My physical movement was slow and deliberate, and my voice weak and strained. Everyone in the family chipped in to take care of me. As soon as I had a bath I would head downstairs, and breakfast would be ready. I would watch telly and doze off for hours in a comfortable recliner chair recently acquired for my convenience and it would be the aroma of lunch that would wake me up. It was a serious pampering and fattening period. Emmanuel and Isaac would take turns at taking me for a walk just so I could stretch my legs. It was hard to keep steady and strong, but I kept at it. Day in and out I was gradually being restored.

I don't know how my wife got contacted by the BBC but within a few days of my being home we were interviewed together live on television during a news segment to discuss our personal experience as a family with the raging pandemic. BBC news online also covered my story on 20th May with the title, *"Coronavirus: Hospital's 'Sickest patient' returns home after weeks in coma."* All of these served to spread the testimony of my healing around in such an incredible way.

The core message was this, 'We were praying to God and we have a large community who joined up with us in prayer, 24 hours a day, people were praying. Our faith kept us positive, and we held on to that.' No matter which platform or opportunity opened for us to tell our story, it was simple and straightforward – God did this.

It Does Not Rain, It Pours

On the 2nd of June, my wife came home with some troubling news. With measured words she explained that something major had happened at the church premises, but she needed for me to be calm and controlled in my reaction. I guess she was afraid I might have a heart attack or something. She then told me an entire section of our church building had collapsed. The roof caved in completely and it was a total loss. Nothing was salvageable. It could have resulted in fatalities but thankfully no one was in that section of the building at that time.

We made our way down to the church and met officials from the fire department, the gas company, the building control department of Milton Keynes Council and a few other people there. They put damage control measures in place to ensure that potential incidents like a fire outbreak, gas leakage or electricity malfunction did not happen to make things worse. It does not rain, it pours. This was not what I needed at a time like this. It was a big blow.

We acquired this building in 2007 and have maintained it with pride since then for the sake of all it means to us; a centre for 'WHOLENESS' especially for many who, for too long, remained noticeably at the margins of society. Holding Forth Christian Centre has been a platform that has given expression and support to many people, Black Africans especially, to actualise their potentials and make a success of their lives and aspirations. Many lives have been touched, many families strengthened, and much credibility gained as an institution of repute and integrity. The section that collapsed was what we called – Victory Hall, the smaller of our two halls.

It was a nicely done up function room used for social events, seminars, receptions, our Sunday school classes, etc. It was a valuable space that complemented our main hall – Covenant Hall, which is our worship sanctuary. The reason for the roof collapse is a long story. The building itself is one structure made up of three sections. The first section, where you have the main sanctuary was built in 1936 but has undergone significant renovation since then.

The middle part is the most recent having been remodelled in 1998 to provide an additional floor which not only provides a foyer area that connects the first and third section but also has facilities like the kitchen, toilets, and offices upstairs. The third section was built in the early 1970s as an adjoining facility to the sanctuary. It is this third section that collapsed.

Structural engineers have determined that the collapse is due to a design fault which stems from a type of roofing/beam support that Building Regulations in the early 70s approved of but are no longer acceptable standards today and have not been since the late 80s and early 90s. Although the entire building itself is fully insured, we are not able to make an insurance claim on this loss for reasons of this technicality and we have not been able to decide on the best way forward in moving past this unfortunate development.

Estimates from Architects about the probable cost of redesigning and rebuilding the hall comes to about half a million pounds! Hopefully, when the disruption this coronavirus pandemic has caused everyone is over, we would be able to explore avenues of fund raising to rebuild this section and bounce back again as a ministry. Our God of signs and wonders can and will do it again. Has he not said in his word, "Your people will rebuild what has long been in ruins, building again on the old foundations. You will be known as the people who rebuilt the walls, who restored the ruined houses." [Isaiah 58 v 12 GNT]

Pressed on every side[22]

A week from the incident at the church, my good friend and colleague in ministry who had been ill for most of 2020 passed away peacefully in his sleep in his house. His death was a sad and painful loss. Like they did for

---

[22] 2 Corinthians 4:8 (KJV) 'We are troubled on every side, yet not distressed; we are perplexed, but not in despair…'

me, the church and others had been praying for his recovery too and the testimony of me back on my feet was a great encouragement that we would see him healed as well. I reckon God saw it differently.

I remember at some point when I was sick of the coronavirus but was still at home isolating and fighting, I was in the presence of God in a dream and was comforted with an assurance I would come out of my affliction. This was before I went to the hospital and everything else that followed. In that dream, the assurance I received that all would be well gave me boldness to make a petition of the Lord about my friend also; I was reminding the Lord he and I still had a lot of work to do and that the testimony of both of us restored to wellness would further the work of the gospel a great deal. I am sure the Lord heard me, but I heard nothing back. He was silent, not a yes or a no.

The encounter felt so real that when I woke up, I told my wife I was sure my friend and I would be fine. But now we have received the opinion of God on the matter and his own definition of 'fine' is not always the way we define it.[23] The first Sunday I was back in church to preach, I went see him after service to encourage him and pray with him. He was happy to see me. He recognised me and said, 'Rev, Hallelujah. We praise God.' I spent a brief time with him and had to leave to allow him rest. That was the last time we would see. He was a true soldier for Christ. Rest in peace my brother.

About this time too, my brother-in-law who lived in Lagos died after a very short stay in the hospital. The hospital was unable to confirm whether it was COVID related or not but the suddenness of it all was very shattering to us as a family. He was buried on Friday 26th June in Iloko – Ijesa, Nigeria. Another good man gone. Adieu. The next day, on Saturday 27th June, in Milton Keynes, I was on hand to coordinate the Service of Songs for my friend and colleague which was via a well-attended ceremony on zoom that lasted for almost three hours. I am including the tribute I paid him on that occasion in honour of his memory.

---

[23] Isaiah 55 v 8 -9 (NLT) "My thoughts are nothing like your thoughts," says the Lord. "And my ways are far beyond anything you could imagine. For just as the heavens are higher than the earth, so my ways are higher than your ways and my thoughts higher than your thoughts."

Tribute to a divine man on a divine mission

The last few months which culminated in the passing of our good friend, brother, and ministry partner, have been very hard for us to bear. Since the relocation of the family to the UK [Milton Keynes] from South Africa, a peculiar and strong bond developed, and our two families literally became like one. Understandably, a shared sense of commitment to ministry and devotion to family values strengthened the cord: for this illustrious servant of God, love for God and family were the most important things in his life and it is hard for us to come to terms with the reality of his passing.

For the few years I had the privilege to work directly with Apostle in ministry, I learnt so much. I gained tremendous insight into the deeper things of God from the wealth of revelation knowledge of biblical truth he had. A strong teacher of the Word, an audacious man of faith, a man of humble and generous spirit, a man undoubtedly on a timed and divine mission. Like Apostle Paul, '[you] have fought a good fight, [you] have finished the race, [you] have kept the faith' and although your voice falls silent in death, the echo of your words will never stop ringing in our ears. Especially your constant reminder to us all that, 'He [God] who has been faithful on six occasions will not fail us on the seventh!'

Thank you for your great life. I will miss our breakfast meetings.

On Monday 29th June, I officiated the funeral ceremony and committal of the body of this dear friend and brother to earth. The work of the Kingdom must go on. Understandably though, all of these took a toll on me physically as my strength was not yet up to par, but I am grateful God gave me the grace and enablement to keep up with all my responsibilities and engagements.

Meanwhile, the relevant hospital departments were making their mandatory follow up calls to check up on how well I was doing in my recovery and rehabilitation process.

On 25th June I received a letter from the Mental Health department of the Hospital,

Dear Mr Ajala

I am writing as a follow up to your recent admission to hospital. We are aware of the potential psychological impact of long stays in ICU during the current pandemic, particularly for patients who experience intense treatment. For some people, they may experience an increase in anxiety or low mood.

For this reason, we agreed to contact you after one month of your discharge from hospital to check in with how you are managing from a psychological point of view. I have attempted to contact you on a couple of occasions however have been unsuccessful.

If you would like to talk about the psychological impact of your experience in hospital, or feel you would like some additional support, please call our office. I would be more than happy to discuss this further with you.

She was unsuccessful in reaching me because I hit the ground running. There were things to attend to and I didn't need psychological support then and I still don't need it now. Daily, I was living in the reality of being upheld by the power of God's word which tells me 'God hath not given us the spirit of fear; but of power, and of love, and of a sound mind.' [2 Tim.1:7 KJV] His word works, and I am still standing.

The physiotherapy department had a list of exercises they suggested to me and required me to do as often as I could. My left arm was weaker than my right one and was achy most mornings when I woke up. I ordered for and received a set of squeeze ball hand exercisers. A squeeze ball is a palm-sized ball that is an excellent therapeutic aid, ideal for helping a user with exercising and strengthening the hand, wrist, or arm. In addition to this, I also tried to increase the length and frequency of my exercise walks.

The physiotherapist was pleased with the efforts I was making and the progress I was showing. We had a few follow up calls and within 6 months of me being discharged she took me off her list of patients to follow up. My rehabilitation effort continued to show increased improvement which, again, was another testimony of God's faithfulness.

Faith and the Omniscience of God

Sunday 7th of June was my first time back on the pulpit since March. It was quite an emotional moment for everyone considering what had happened in the intervening period. The viewership number of those who joined us for this service, online, was the largest we ever recorded. People wanted to hear what message I may have to share with the world about encounters from where I had been. I hope they were not disappointed that day. And if they were, I hope this book is enough compensation.

My sermon that day was *'Perspective and the challenge of faith.'* I believe God laid it on my heart to address this topic because the issue of the coronavirus pandemic affected the faith of many people in the body of Christ generally. Again, that age-old question of why a good God would allow so much suffering and disruption was not far from the minds of many. Closer to home, there were some whose faith was shaken as they wondered why God had allowed his servant to go through such an ordeal. Aren't we, as children of God supposed to be shielded from such evil? There were yet others, though, whose faith was strengthened the more in a God who showed up and answered the prayers of his children and brought victory out of what was imminent defeat. Either way, it is easy to see that perspective is key.

To my mind, a correct approach to faith issues is to adopt a perspective that predisposes 'God will' rather than 'will not' come through for us in any given situation while at the same time recognise, we cannot force God to act as and when we want him to. If he did, he would no longer be God. Faith requires that we trust God. And we do. But then God has the prerogative to do as he pleases because he knows and sees everything [all sides, every time] while we only see and know in part[s].

When God tested Abraham and asked him to sacrifice his son, Isaac, there was no way he could be 100% sure what the outcome of that instruction was going to be. Yet he trusted God. That was faith in action.

[Heb.11 v 17 -19 NLT]
It was by faith that Abraham offered Isaac as a sacrifice when God was testing him. Abraham, who had received God's promises, was ready to sacrifice his only son, Isaac, even though God had told him, "Isaac is the son through whom your descendants will be counted." Abraham reasoned that if Isaac died, God was able to bring him back to life again. And in a sense, Abraham did receive his son back from the dead.

Abraham's perspective was that he was going to leave the eventual outcome up to God. Faith is not believing God for what we want; It is believing that God will do or has done what he wants which is in our better interest either way. In the words of the songwriter, 'In our living or in our dying,' true faith says, 'All, all is well.' This is the perspective we ought to have when we talk about having faith in God. There is an important lesson for us in the example Abraham shows,

[Gen. 22 v 5 KJV]
"Stay here with the donkey," Abraham told the servants. "The boy and I will travel a little farther. We will worship there, and then we will come right back."

Could Abraham have been so sure he and the lad would return? No. Can we ever be sure about the outcome of an event or situation just because we have faith and exercise same? No. How much faith is enough faith? The challenge of faith is that it cannot be gauged in us as one would do for petrol in a car for example. How do I know I have 'enough' faith and how do I know if what I have will suffice for what a particular situation might require? Above and beyond all these, how can one know the limit or extent, or nature of the test God is willing to take one through?

Will God save or help me at the beginning, middle or end of my trial, testing, or situation? Or will he, like he did at resurrection, come through after every weapon of the enemy including death has left its mark and done its worst? Faith in God is not about when or how He intervenes but about us believing and accepting that any outcome He allows is perfect and is for our good.

Concerning the heroes of faith, recorded in Hebrews chapter 11, it is said in verse 13, [NLT]

All these people died still believing what God had promised them. They did not receive what was promised, but they saw it all from a distance and welcomed it. They agreed that they were foreigners and nomads here on earth.

One is saddened by the fact that what ought to be a correct perspective on faith has been impaired by the error of name it, claim it, receive it; a culture the church today has mindlessly embraced. When I resigned myself to being put on the ventilator it was not because I abandoned faith or that I had given up on God's ability to save me from a situation that gives just a 50:50 chance of survival. Not at all. I had faith, and so did many others around me, that God was able to choose when and how he would intervene in the matter. And he did.

The perspective we hold, as Christians, on matters like this is important because it influences our actions in many respects. Currently, many Christians wonder whether to take the coronavirus vaccination or not. Personally, I believe this is a moot point. In my case, God stepped in before a coronavirus vaccine was even developed. Whether one takes the vaccination or not, God is the one who decides the length of our days not anyone or anything else. Yet, a perspective that sees vaccination or any form of medical intervention, for that matter, as something that compromises our faith in God is faulty.

For each one of us, God knows the race he has set for us and the path he has put us on which, again, is where the issue of faith and assurance comes in. Assurance in a loving father who is working it all out for our good and for his own glory. However else others choose to see it, I see my entire experience with COVID as a situation which God has used to stretch our faith, test our resolve, and get us down on our knees praying. It has also served as opportunity for God to show us what his grace of mercy looks like and in doing so, re-educate and refocus our mind to what authentic and real faith in Him is.

God knows what he is doing all the time. Even if or when this fact does not seem obvious to you, have faith in God no matter what, and never let your [own] understanding of how things are going or unfolding change your perspective about the reliability and almightiness and goodness of God.

"But the God of all grace, who hath called us unto his eternal glory by Christ Jesus, after that ye have suffered a while, make you perfect, stablish, strengthen, settle you."

- *The Bible [I Peter 5: 10 KJV]*

Epilogue

God is [Still] at Work

Since my recovery, I have been meditating on what possible new assignment(s) God might have for me. I still pastor the church in Milton Keynes, but I feel there is something more. Something different. I know there must be a larger purpose to be served by reason of this second chance on life God has given me. It feels like one race is accomplished and that I am at the starting bloc of a different race. Whether the race ahead is a sprint, or a marathon is yet unknown but that the sands of time is running out for all of us is not in doubt.

God must have brought me out unscathed from the clutches of COVID-19 for a reason. I say unscathed because there are many people who have survived the coronavirus but still suffer long term effects from contracting it.

According to a NHS bulletin, *'there are lots of symptoms you can have after a coronavirus infection. Common long COVID symptoms include extreme tiredness (fatigue), shortness of breath, chest pain or tightness, problems with memory and concentration ("brain fog"), difficulty sleeping (insomnia), heart palpitations, dizziness, pins and needles, joint pain, depression and anxiety, tinnitus, earaches, feeling sick, diarrhoea, stomach aches, loss of appetite, a high temperature, cough, headaches, sore throat, changes to sense of smell or taste, rashes ...'*

To the glory of God, I do not experience any of these symptoms. God, in his mercy has made me completely whole again. My situation reminds me of what the bible said about the three Hebrew men, Shadrach, Meshach, and Abednego, after God brought them out of the fiery furnace. It is said,

> [Dan. 4 v 26 – 27 NLT]
> *...that the fire had not touched them. Not a hair on their heads was singed, and their clothing was not scorched. They didn't even smell of smoke!*

God has been very kind and merciful to me indeed. I have not been physically, mentally, or emotionally diminished in any way despite the trauma of the recent past. A few months into my rehabilitation phase I went in by appointment to see my Doctor for a face-to-face follow- up clinic consultation. Below are extracts from his report,

> *Today Mr Ajala came to the Critical Care follow-up with his wife, Esther.*
>
> *Physical:*
> *He describes his physical condition as 90% back to his previous best. He is walking 7 kilometres every day and does not get shortness of breath with moderate or even fairly severe exertion. When he was first discharged from hospital, he said he was about 50% of his best in terms of his physicality. He described his hands as being particularly painful and was really unable to write for about a month after discharge. He is also describing his nails as being particularly discoloured and ridged, although his skin is fine.*
>
> *Psychological:*
> *In terms of his psychology, Mr Ajala describes he was initially disorientated post extubation, but very rapidly came back to normal. He has never had nightmares or flashbacks and has been sleeping relatively normally, both in his ward stay in hospital as well as at home. His focus and concentration seem good, and he describes his memory as normal. He has been back at work as a Pastor since June with weekly sermons.*
>
> *Overall, Mr Ajala has suffered a very significant critical illness and has recovered from it remarkably well, both psychologically and physically. He has received exercises from our Physiotherapist to do at home, but he has been managing exceptionally well with the exercise programme that he set himself and I have suggested that he continues that progress but does not get frustrated when he can't quite do everything he wants to because although his progress has been remarkable, it will still take him a little bit of time to get back to his previous best.*
>
> *It was truly lovely to see Mr Ajala and his wife, Esther at our follow-up clinic looking as well as he did.*

Two months into my rehabilitation (July 2020), I remember praying for acceleration in the pace of my recovery even though, up to that point, I was already making good progress. Two weeks or so, after my discharge, I was independent enough to do everything I needed to do by myself. My prayer at this point was therefore for full restoration.

I desired, for instance, to increase my capacity for longer walks and for consistency in doing same. In his faithfulness, I received the grace to do this and everyday throughout the month of August I walked consistently for at least 90mins. During this time, I floated the idea among church members of 'Movemore: Livemore' as I tried to persuade more people to get on-board the fitness train and commit to daily long walks. Only a few people bought into the idea.

Since that time, I have developed a liking for the outdoors averaging even longer distances as often as I can. I added intermittent jogging to brisk long walks, and along routes with mixed topography to add to the effectiveness of the fitness efforts. I did say to the nurse while I was in the ICU, I would run a marathon and she reckoned my comment was part of the stupor induced by the coma. Although I am yet to run a marathon, I am on track to achieve the level of wellness and fitness I had imagined for myself back when I could not even lift my hands and legs. So far so good. All through the months, I have kept my determination going; out there on the trail, kitted as occasion required. Along with my regular fitness efforts and my religious observances, I try to eat well, sleep well, worry less, but contemplate more.

In many ways, I feel like an athlete preparing for an important sporting event. I am not sure exactly what is ahead, but I am waiting on God to speak to me as clearly as he did in 1995 when he asked, "Are you ready to do the work I have for you to do…?" My affirmative response at that time led to the start of Holding Forth the Word Ministry. The rest, as they say, is history. The Lord knows my answer to any commission he gives will always be -Yes Lord. I am just patiently waiting on a clear word about what the 'new' work is. Until then, I am fully back to my duties in my local assembly where, since the first week of June 2020, I have led as busy a schedule as is possible given the circumstances of lockdown andthe restrictions that come with it.

The past one year has not been easy on us all. Families have been stretched and tested in many areas. Many have lost loved ones, their homes, their jobs, etc., and many are at the verge of losing their minds. The full impact of the lockdown and isolation on the mental health of people remains to be seen even as the toll of this situation on pastors has become very high due to increased counselling needs among people we feel accountable for. Someone sent me a text that read,

> 'Hello pastor. What a year! I find myself thinking hard. I don't know what lies ahead. It's scary at times and I'm very sober.'

He is not alone. The text echoes the heart of millions out there who feel this same way – scared and sober! The question is, where do we go from here? My answer is simple: To God. We go to God. My response to the text was this,

> 'It's sober times for everyone my dear brother. The rich and the not so rich. There is something out there bigger than us all reminding us of our vulnerability. We must seek to find purpose within the plan of God. I am not talking about being in church ministry but about touching lives meaningfully starting from where you are. Doing all the good that you can do. A kind word. A glass of water to those who need it. It is a tough world out there and it's getting tougher because people have stood decency and values upside down.'

The truth we need to know is that we can only find rest, meaning, purpose and fulfilment in God through a closer walk with Christ. As Christ himself said, [John 6 v 63 NLT] 'The Spirit alone gives eternal life. Human effort accomplishes nothing. And the very words I have spoken to you are spirit and life.' Unfortunately, this is not the answer the world wants to hear neither is it the counsel the world is ready for. I want you to remember though, that whenever you feel out of your depth in any area of life, the mercy of God and the power of God in his word is always available to you.

When life situations drain you of peace and joy, the mercy of God will reach you and give you the help and assistance you need, filling you with love and strength each new day. Amen.

'The greatest victories are the victories of faith. It is not so much what we can do that counts, but what we can trust God to do.'

- *Author Unknown*

Mercy Said No Indeed.

If you would like to give in support of our efforts,
we suggest donating to:

'HFWM: BUILDING FUND A/C'
Ref:MSNo. Natwest. Acct 60566256
Sortcode 601455